EDMUND WILSON

THE MAN AND HIS WORK

Edited by John Wain

New York · New York University Press · 1978

'*The Poetry of Edmund Wilson*' by Clive James, commissioned for this collection of essays, has recently been published in The New Review.

'*Wilson's Fiction: a Personal Account*' by John Updike is based on an article originally published in The New Republic.

New York University Press
Washington Square, New York, N.Y.10003

'The Great Anachronism: a View from the Sixties' is © 1978 by Alfred Kazin. The contributions by Edith Oliver, Angus Wilson, Bette Crouse Mele, Larzer Ziff, Peter Sharratt, Helen Muchnic, David Flusser, Andrew Harvey and John Wain are © 1978 by Phaidon Press Limited, Oxford.

Library of Congress Catalog Card Number: 78-53094
ISBN 0-8147-9183-2

Printed in Great Britain

mw 3/79 69/4

Contents

The Contributors

DAVID FLUSSER is Professor of Comparative Religion at the Hebrew University of Jerusalem. He gave crucial help to Edmund Wilson in his study of the Dead Sea Scrolls.

ANDREW HARVEY is a Fellow of All Souls College, Oxford. He is engaged on a study of madness in Shakespeare, and is the author of a book of poems, *Masks and Faces* (1977).

CLIVE JAMES, poet, critic, satirist, entertainer. His most recent publications are *Visions before Midnight* (a collection of his television criticism) and a book of verse letters, *Fan-Mail*.

ALFRED KAZIN is Distinguished Professor of English at the State University of New York. He came to prominence with *On Native Grounds* (1942). He has written many books since, including *The Inmost Leaf*, *Contemporaries*, *The Bright Book of Life*; he has published two volumes of autobiography, *A Walker in the City*, and *Starting Out in the Thirties*, and is engaged on a third, from which the present memoir is taken.

BETTE CROUSE MELE is an enrolled member of the Seneca Nation, born on the Allegany Reservation, New York State. Her Seneca name is Gwē-wǎ-nǎ-stāh – Hawk Clan. She is the first Indian and first woman to be President of the Indian Rights Association, Philadelphia. She is on the Board and Executive Committee of *Americans for Indian Opportunity*.

HELEN MUCHNIC is Professor Emeritus of Russian Literature, Smith College. Her publications include: *Dostoevsky's English Reputation, 1881–1936*, *An Introduction to Russian Literature*, *From Gorky to Pasternak*, *Russian Writers: Notes and Essays*.

EDITH OLIVER is a member of the editorial staff of *The New Yorker*, where she works in the books department and reviews off-Broadway plays.

PETER SHARRATT is a lecturer in French at Edinburgh University. His main interest is in French and Latin literature of the sixteenth century; he has written many articles, edited a symposium on *The French Renaissance, 1540–70*, and discovered some unknown poems by Ronsard.

JOHN UPDIKE was born in Shillington, Pennsylvania, and after graduating from Harvard spent a year at the Ruskin School of Fine Art, Oxford. He is the author of some twenty books, including eight novels, and frequently contributes criticism to the *New Yorker*.

JOHN WAIN, poet, novelist, critic, biographer, autobiographer, dramatist, has published some twenty books in the last twenty years; he has taught at universities in England, the United States and France; and he is currently Professor of Poetry at the University of Oxford.

ANGUS WILSON, novelist, critic, Professor of English Literature at the University of East Anglia. He is the author of many famous novels, including *Hemlock and After*, *The Middle Age of Mrs. Eliot*, *Late Call*, *As If By Magic*; of studies of Zola and Dickens; and, most recently, of *The Strange Ride of Rudyard Kipling* (1977).

LARZER ZIFF has written extensively on a range of periods and a number of aspects of American literary culture. Among his books are *The American 1890s* and *Puritanism in America*.

Preface

In 1933, Bernard Shaw gave a lecture from the stage of the Metropolitan Opera House, New York. Edmund Wilson was in the audience; and, in his report of the evening, he tried to convey to readers of a younger generation what it had been like to be young when G.B.S. was first coruscating on to the world stage, and how it was that now, at thirty-eight, he still found that Shaw's 'form had not yet lost All its original brightness, nor appeared Less than archangel ruined':

> Here in this black arrowy figure, this lovely cultivated voice, is the spirit which for those of us who were young when Shaw had reached the height of his power, permeated our minds for a time, stirring new intellectual appetites, exciting our sense of moral issues, sharpening the focus of our vision on the social relations of our world till we could see it as a vividly lit stage full of small, distinct, intensely conceived characters explaining their positions to one another. It was an explanation that burned like a poem. And here is the poet still burning.

Those few lines appear to me to describe Wilson's work as aptly as Shaw's. Where else, in our time, has there been such a master of 'the explanation that burns like a poem'? (He also wrote some poems that read like explanations, but that is forgivable.)

This book is an expression of our gratitude to Edmund Wilson: for existing, and for being Edmund Wilson. The only way to express that gratitude is to take him seriously. He had an enormous range of interests, was a staunch generalist, despised the narrow specialization that crept in during his lifetime. We, who have lived to see that specialization blight every area of our intellectual life, should appreciate that. Where there used to be scholars, there are now experts, who never raise their eyes above the fence surrounding their 'field'. There is actually – I promise you, though I know I shall not be believed – a tutor in English literature at Oxford, yes, actually a Fellow of an Oxford College, who refuses to discuss Shakespeare on the grounds that 'I don't teach the Renaissance'. An English teacher! At Oxford!! Who refuses to discuss Shakespeare!!! Those exclamation marks are expressions of despair.

To this despair Edmund Wilson never succumbed. He went where his interests led him, and he expected to have a readership that was game to go along. From first to last, he addressed that public whom the great critics have always addressed: the community of thoughtful, literate men and women. To them, this book also is addressed; though most of the contributors are, inevitably, more concentrated each in his own field than Wilson had to be. When an amateur makes such bold incursions into fields normally tilled by professionals, his total achievement can most profitably be assessed by assembling a string of these professionals (taking care, of course, to screen out those whose *déformation professionnelle* is on quite the scale of that of the Oxford tutor mentioned above). Thus the play of Wilson's mind over each area is here discussed by someone who normally inhabits that area. Here and there, the provocative liveliness of Wilson's mind pushes a contributor into dissent, into answering back; Andrew Harvey – our youngest collaborator, who was an undergraduate at the time of Wilson's death – takes issue with Wilson's views on poetry and carries on the argument as if Wilson were still there to be argued against, drawing his illustrations often from books published since Wilson died, keeping the argument alive in a way that testifies to the continuing power and stimulus of the man's presence.

Nobody in this volume is here to praise Edmund Wilson and leave it at that. His work, and his personality, were designed for combat. But we argue against him as we argue against a beloved father, an uncle, an elder brother. Some of the contributors to this book worked with Edmund Wilson closely for years. Some knew him tangentially. Others never met him at all, except in the pages of his books. But that third category can never be underestimated; because that is where he remains, where we can all meet him, where his life and his work, his struggles and enjoyments and outrages, will go on.

This book, then, is written for the reader whom Wilson himself addressed – the alert, concerned, intelligent person who wants to understand things, to get the best out of literature and out of life. To such a reader, we say: take this book, live with it, use it: it will help you to an understanding of one of this century's truly remarkable men. And when you understand him, he will become your friend. And once he is your friend, the world will never again seem a dull place.

1977   John Wain

EDMUND WILSON
THE MAN

EDITH OLIVER

Notes on a Marginal Friendship

The excitement, the candor, the generosity, the decibels – those are the first words that come to mind as I think about Edmund Wilson – the first, though not, of course, the only ones. The excitement was something that he both felt himself and aroused in others. Seldom could there have been a more powerful, better stocked, or more ravenous mind, yet it was not simply the intellectual strength of his critiques and reviews that could literally make one pace the floor in the middle of a piece about, say, Ulysses S. Grant (of all people); it was Wilson's own enthusiasm that came pouring through the type. No matter what the assignment, no matter what the book or subject under discussion, Wilson was always the *reader* – never the explainer, the expert, the 'professor'. (He once used that word to contemptuously describe another critic.) This was partly a matter of breeding, I think – of old-fashioned good manners: one spoke or wrote *to* people not *at* them. In any case, it was as a fellow-reader or a reporter that he shared his enthusiasm for merit, wherever it occurred, and his own thrill at discovery. He was, as far as I know, the first English-speaking critic to 'discover' that remarkable French-Canadian novelist Marie-Claire Blais, when no other English-speaking critic was paying the slightest attention to the literature of French Canada. It was he who (again, as far as I know) first discovered – or, more exactly, first put to use, in a piece of literary detection - a fact that had long been buried in medical history: that Oscar Wilde had contracted syphilis as a young man. From this Wilson proposed that Wilde had thought himself cured and had married and then, when he found he was still infected, had broken off sexual

3

relations with his wife and become exclusively homosexual.

Wilson never denied his prejudices, of which he had as many as the next man, or tried to pass them off as judgements or opinions. 'I am a Hispanophobe,' he said one day, summarily terminating a conversation with a *New Yorker* writer who was trying proudly but vainly to show him snapshots of a summer cottage in Majorca. He was always forthright: 'Somebody new is doing your dresses. Very good. Very becoming. Changes you.' Extraordinarily interested in anything that interested him at all, he absolutely shut out anything that didn't ('She *bores* me', he would say with finality, and from him the word 'insipid' was lethal), and he could smell pretense and fakery seven leagues off.

Acquaintanceship was not Edmund Wilson's métier; friendship was – friendship wholehearted and staunch. Our friendship, though it was wholehearted enough (on both sides, I like to think), was also perforce marginal, since it was based upon his relatively infrequent visits to *The New Yorker*, where I've worked in the book-review department since the early fifties – a scattering of lunches at the Princeton Club when he came in from Wellfleet or Talcottville to turn in a manuscript, dinners and drinks at the Algonquin, where he never ceased to fight with the waiters about the size of the check ('But we didn't eat any bread.' . . . 'You've added it up wrong; it's *much* less'), and a couple of forays into the theatre.

> There are few things I enjoy so much as talking to people about books which I have read and they haven't, and making them wish they had – preferably a book that is hard to get or in a language that they do not know.
> 'A Weekend at Ellerslie', reprinted in
> *The Shores of Light* (1952)

Our friendship was a slow developer. For the first year or so, I was so numb with awe, so unfocussed in his presence, that I could hardly hear what he was saying – forgetting that shyness, of course, works both ways. Then one day he was sitting beside my desk groping for some *mot juste* or other, and I timidly offered 'lousy'. 'Yes, lousy!' he said, and that did it – first names from then on, and funny memos and drawings and notes, and comments on my mail, which he read without shame as it lay open on my desk. But until then I was on the receiving end of a lot of that literary gamesmanship he describes in 'A Weekend at Ellerslie' and all I can remember, during those early months, is saying over and over 'I'm afraid I've never read that, Mr. Wilson,' or 'I'm sorry, but I've never heard of him'. Then, as things grew more comfortable, the literary showing off became so entertaining and charming that I was tempted to pretend I hadn't read a book just in the hope of setting off an eruption. Most of the time he was right. 'Never read *Virgin Soil*? Call yourself a cultivated woman!' he cried once. I hadn't and don't. So we made a bargain.

'You can buy me *Virgin Soil*,' I said, 'if I can buy you *Lucky Jim*.'

'What's that?'

'You'll see.' Immeasurable benefit to both of us, and *The New Yorker* got a splendid essay on Kingsley Amis when *That Uncertain Feeling* appeared. How Wilson relished humor, how he responded to quality! He knew either everything or nothing at all about an author or a subject, and I once had the (unworthy) delight of hearing him ask, 'Who is Brendan Behan?' (You call yourself a cultivated man!) That exchange led to our going to a revival of *The Hostage* in a minuscule theatre in Greenwich Village. He took to Behan at once and, as usual, forthrightly. 'Greatest talent since Sean O'Casey!' he shouted in the midst of the performance, and the actors froze in place and stared.

But the thing I have particularly felt is the difference between the general tone, the psychological and literary atmosphere, of the period – the twenties and early thirties – when most of these pieces of Mrs. Parker's were written, and the atmosphere of the present time. It was suddenly brought home to me how much freer people were – in their emotion, in their ideas, and in expressing themselves. In the twenties they could love, they could travel, they could stay up late at night as extravagantly as they pleased; they could think or say or write whatever seemed to them amusing or interesting.

'A Toast and a Tear for Dorothy Parker', *The New Yorker*, (1944); reprinted in *Classics and Commercials* (1950)

There is more than even chance that Edmund Wilson, at forty-nine, never realized that it wasn't people in *the* twenties so much as people in *their* twenties who could still love and travel and stay up late at night as extravagantly as they pleased, but otherwise the quote stands up: in a sense, Wilson never left the nineteen-twenties and the freedom to pursue whatever seemed to him amusing or interesting.

'I have a free evening in town. What shall I see?'

'Mike Nichols and Elaine May.'

Next morning: 'I've just done something I haven't done in twenty-five years; I've sent roses to an actress.'

When a beautiful woman gives a beautiful performance, what one does – or did – of course, is send roses. He also hoped that the flowers would serve as an introduction when he returned to the theatre the following evening, although I hope I convinced him that if he just sent his name backstage, Miss May would be unlikely to slam her dressing-room door in his face. The result of that encounter was that he had many delightful suppers with both Miss May and Mr. Nichols after many performances. When the show closed and the partnership broke up, he continued to see a great deal of Mr. Nichols, in and out of town – advising, chivying, and administering his own incomparable encouragement. 'An Open Letter to Mike Nichols' serves as an afterword to Wilson's *The Duke of Palermo and other Plays* (1969), and in it he wrote, 'You are something of a theatrical genius with an intelligence and imagination together with an ability to make them effective which are excessively rare on Broadway', ending, 'If God were not thought to be dead, I should beg Him to speed you, my boy, and to preserve you from the fleshpots of Hollywood.'

The candor. He gave candor, and expected it, in a way that, come to think of it, does seem a little out of date. One could say anything to him about his own work. E. B. White once protested to him that it was outrageous to make changes in the early diaries that Wilson was starting to publish, and I remember Wilson thundering back, 'Nonsense! Nonsense! Nothing dishonest about improving one's work!' Most of the time, disagreement truly interested him, and his responses to it were pure and forceful. After asking me once about an article that his former wife, Mary McCarthy, had just written, he was astonished when I protested that I couldn't discuss her work with him. 'Too embarrassing,' I said. 'Embarrassing!' he said. 'What does that mean? I have never known what that word meant.' He felt that anything in print – and, for all I know, out of it – was discussable. Any piece of writing, whatever its provenance or circumstances, could be dealt with truthfully, even bluntly. In 1922, he wrote of Scott Fitzgerald, even then one of his closest friends,

> In short, one of the chief weaknesses of *This Side of Paradise* is that it is really not *about* anything; its intellectual and moral content amounts to little more than a gesture – a gesture of indefinite revolt. The story itself, furthermore, is very immaturely imagined: it is always just verging on the ludicrous. And, finally, *This Side of Paradise* is one of the most illiterate books of any merit ever published (a fault which the publisher's proofreader seems to have made no effort to remedy). Not only is it ornamented with bogus ideas and faked literary references, but it is full of literary words tossed about with the most reckless inaccuracy.
>
> I have said that *This Side of Paradise* commits almost every sin that a novel can possibly commit, but it does not commit the unpardonable sin: it does not fail to live. The whole preposterous farrago is animated with life.

And Wilson finished up exactly as he started. One of the last letters I had from him, dated 2 January 1971, ended with a postscript about E. M. Forster: 'Your friend E. M. Forster's *Maurice* is not only his worst novel but one of the worst ever written by a reputable writer.'

His opinions, it goes without saying, were strong, and they

increased in strength with the double Scotches and the vodka martinis. (His capacity for booze was impressive, though perhaps not quite as impressive as he thought it was as the years crept on.) The opinions – especially concerning people at *The New Yorker* – could be wrong as often as they were right (if wrong and right have any meaning in this context). He once referred to the late Harold Ross as an 'ignoramus,' and it took him years to get the full measure of William Shawn's extraordinary character and accomplishment. Rogers Whitaker, who edited his copy, found him so difficult to handle that he was flabbergasted when I repeated a compliment that Wilson had paid him; Wilson had apparently never given him the slightest indication of his esteem and confidence. Wilson's opinions that I was most likely to hear were those concerning *New Yorker* staff writers and the magazine itself. During the years I knew him, he never seemed at home at the magazine (or, for that matter in New York itself, which exhausted him); for one thing, he could never understand the well-known lack of camaraderie in these austere corridors, though friendships run deep here, too. Perhaps he was too *innocent* to realize that his very eminence and occasional brusqueness of manner could frighten and put off people who might want to ask him out for a drink or lunch or drop into the office he happened to be occupying. Of course, he could see that Joseph Mitchell and a number of other writers were 'first-rate,' but he thought little of quite a few, and the unfavorable pronouncements were, as likely as not, delivered in ringing tones in public places. 'That book review you ran was an absolute disgrace. How could you assign a book like that to a girl like ——,' he would call down the hall to me, referring to an unfortunate young woman who shall be nameless, since I cannot share Wilson's views on embarrassment. Or, of a certain critic, reverberatingly named, 'No taste! None at all! Unreadable!' Or, most characteristically, a simple pronouncement of the offending name, followed by a contemptuous guttural grunt of dismissal. He could be a holy terror.

There was another side to that innocence, though. I doubt whether he had the slightest idea of how welcome he was to other writers or how generous they thought him. He himself was one of the few writers I have ever met who were entirely free of envy.

8

There was none of that envy of youth that is so prevalent among the aging, and nothing sour or embittered ever impeded his generosity to those who were starting out. As it was with Mike Nichols, so it was with our brilliant young critic, the late Donald Malcolm, whom he insisted upon meeting and praising.

Many people have written that in men of genius the child is somehow completely preserved in the man. That was surely true of Wilson. His interest in magic and tricks and puzzles and jokes and puppetry were lifelong, and he was a very good puppeteer. One evening, he and Elena Wilson and I went down to the Village to see the Bil Baird puppeteers and then, after the show, went backstage to examine all the paraphernalia, and then upstairs to Mr. Baird's apartment. Another guest that evening was a famous Hungarian puppeteer, whom Wilson had wanted for years to meet, and who, it turned out, had wanted to meet Wilson for just as long. He and Wilson and Baird moved off into a corner, talking in inaudible, impassioned tones about the subject so mysteriously dear to their hearts, while Elena Wilson and I waited, with a patience that comes more naturally to her than it does to me. But Wilson had a wonderful time, and the two other men said that meeting him had been a lifelong dream come true. His Christmas cards were pamphlets of poems and rebuses and puzzles and funny quatrains and limericks, and on Valentine's Day one was almost certain to find a mysterious letter which, when opened, released a paper butterfly on a spring. In a London record shop I once found a repressing of the songs of old music-hall stars. It was pretty terrible, the voices sounding far away through the scratches and surface noises, but one of the stars was Dan Leno, who had always been a very romantic figure to me. So I bought several copies of the record and sent one to Wilson. In his letter of thanks, he agreed that the record was poor, but said that he, too, was delighted to hear Leno, however faintly, because although he had heard many of the other performers when he was taken to London as a boy, he had missed Leno and had always been curious about him. He promised that the next time he came to town he would sing the songs he remembered, and describe the singers. And so he did. The voice had, as they say, gone, but the lyrics had not, and for over an hour, sitting in the tip-back chair in my office, he sang the words made famous by Little Tich and Vesta Victoria and George Robey and Albert Chevalier, among others, resurrecting a kind of theatre that has now vanished, and unconsciously resurrecting himself as well – the enraptured boy sitting in the audience and seizing every detail. He mimicked the characterizations and described the costumes – even, by hearsay, the characterization and the costume of the never-seen Leno in his role as a spindly Beefeater guiding a party of tourists through the Tower of London. Marie Lloyd was the star he loved and remembered best, and he all but brought her back to life, singing her numbers, imitating her spirited, luscious Cockney and the sly, deft way she handled her pocketbook and other props.

And, finally, the decibels. Perhaps I am wrong to speak of them last, because today, summoning Edmund Wilson up, I hear him before I see him. The singing voice may have cracked, but the speaking voice had not. Wonderful, piercing, and resonant – even at the end, when he was so frail and ill – it carried from one floor of the office to the next. Oh, hooray! Edmund's back in town!

ALFRED KAZIN

The Great Anachronism: a View from the Sixties

In a stained old Panama hat, the long white dress shirt that he wore everywhere – 'I have only one way of dressing' – brown Bermuda shorts that bulged with his capacious middle, and carrying a handsome straight gold-topped cane that had been long in his family, Edmund Wilson, having been driven by his wife Elena, now walked slowly, with some difficulty, along the edge of the great ocean beach at Wellfleet in Cape Cod. Finished with his long daily stint, he was now ready to look at Nature and have a talk.

The beach was full of interesting and notable people to talk to. There on the beach, any August afternoon in the mid-1960s, could be seen Arthur and Marian Schlesinger, Gilbert Seldes, Allen Tate and Isabella Gardner, Edwin and Veniette O'Connor, Richard and Beatrice Hofstadter, Robert and Betty Jean Lifton, Irving and Arien Howe, Harry and Elena Levin, Daniel and Janet Aaron. At times there could also be seen Stuart and Suzanne Hughes, Jason and Barbara Epstein, Philip and Maggie Roth, Marcel and Constance Breuer. Once there was a view of Svetlana, daughter of Stalin, accompanied by the Georgian writer Chacavadze, whose wife was a Romanoff and who herself often modestly made her way to the South Wellfleet Post office to receive letters from her cousins in Buckingham Palace. It was said that Svetlana and Mrs. Chacavadze had even compared notes on what it was like to live in the Kremlin.

The beach was full of television producers, government and U.N. 'advisers' – social scientists, psychohistorians, professors by the dozen – people all definitely 'in'. There was so much important, authoritative writing going on in Wellfleet that one professor's wife, trying to hush the neighborhood children, put her head out of the window and said pleadingly to the children: 'Professor X is writing a book review. I'm sure all your fathers and mothers have reviews to write too!' The children of another writer, left to themselves on the beach, were playing a game with a ball devised by the witty novelist Edwin O'Connor. It was called 'Schlesinger', and consisted of trying to knock over a beer can propped up on a little sand hill. If you failed the number of times there were letters in *Schlesinger*, you had to pay a forfeit thought up at the last moment by O'Connor, but which invariably consisted in walking around some of the lesser discussion groups on the beach and mocking the Hungarian psychoanalyst and the graphic designer from Yale.

O'Connor enjoyed jossing 'the heavy intellectual set' – there were so few other novelists about. But making fun of Schlesinger was not making fun of Jack Kennedy and the New Frontier. O'Connor could not have been prouder of his fellow 'Irishman'; no one else on that beach mourned him so sincerely and was still enjoying the 1960s so much. In his first days in Wellfleet Ed O'Connor had gone about on a bicycle. *The Last Hurrah*, that successful and hilarious novel of the last great Irish politico in Boston, had made him rich. He now had a beautifully severe *avant-garde* house in the Wellfleet woods built for him by a haughty Russian-born architect, who never arrived on the beach without two enormous, madly restive, threatening German shepherds who frightened everyone around while his master, who had an icy Oxford accent and the majesty of a Diaghilev, could be heard knocking down everyone else's political universe. From time to time he was an advanced liberal.

Dwight Macdonald was divorced from Nancy and no longer came to Wellfleet. Mary McCarthy and Bowden Broadwater had hung on long after her divorce from Edmund Wilson. But after writing *A Charmed Life* about Wellfleet and divorcing Broadwater, she had departed for Paris and Maine. But Nicholas and Mike Macdonald and Reuel Wilson could be seen in a crowd of other Wellfleet young people – Phillipses, of the family that had once owned most of this beachfront, these dunes and the lakes behind them; young Mansons, grandchildren of the old American socialists William English Walling and Rose Strunsky.

Wellfleet, just a few miles down from where Provincetown spread over the tip of the Cape, was not as famous for writers and rebellions as Provincetown. It had no rebellions and no rebels. Its first notable summer folk were architects and designers from the Bauhaus, its next psychoanalysts. By now it was distinctly, as the pretentious consort of a famous historian put it, *la plage des intellectuels*. It was indeed. By now there seemed to be a book for every day of American history. The universities and the mass media had joined in incessantly producing still more documentation of 'just what makes us tick' and 'our American heritage'. Nothing 'American' was alien to the incessant cultural analysts and psycho-historians, many of them of recent immigrant stock, who each summer in Wellfleet held seminars and read papers at each other, endlessly fascinated by the wealth of material to which they felt happily related by their newfound status as academic authorities and advisers to government.

Edmund Wilson, who lived in Wellfleet the year round, hated it in summer and called it 'the fucking Riviera'. Oddly, Wilson was one of the few 'old radicals' in Wellfleet, along with his friend Charlie Walker, the old Greek scholar and labor historian. I had first seen Wilson in Provincetown in 1940; he was carefully bicycling to the Portuguese bakery. He bought his crazily ranging house in Wellfleet before the main Cape highway, Route 6, had been laid out past his door. That was long before *la plage des intellectuels* had settled into Wellfleet as a continuation of Cambridge, New Haven, the Institute for Advanced Study and the executive assistants' wing of the White House. I had met Wilson in 1942, when he was married to Mary McCarthy and already isolated from fashionable opinion by his obstinate isolationism. I had met him again in London, at the end of the war, at a great party given for him by the Ministry of Information when he was on his way to Italy and Greece as a roving correspondent for the *New Yorker*. He was still against the war, still bitterly suspicious of the English. True to his own 'British' delight in being difficult, he was turning a cold face to the many writers who had come to pay him homage and amazed me by his appeal: 'We must stick together against these Limeys.'

Wilson's arrival on the Wellfleet beach regularly caused a stir. A definite mental avidity and nervous unrest fixed itself around his bulky antique figure. He was so definitely not of this time, of these younger people, this academic set. The sight of him in his Panama hat and well-filled Bermuda shorts, the cane propped up in the sand like a sword in declaration of war, instantly brought out in me the mingled anxiety and hilarity that I used to feel watching Laurel and Hardy about to cross a precipice. There was so much mischief, disdain and intellectual solemnity wrapped up behind that get-up, that high, painfully distinct voice, that lonely proud face. His immense authority for everyone on this beach – especially among the literary professors who explained to their classes that Wilson was not 'really a critic at all' – was clearly at odds with the too-elegant cane, the stains so carefully preserved on the Panama hat, the absurdly formal long white shirt sometimes flopping over the bulky stomach in the Bermuda shorts. He was a 'character'. The improbably loud high voice – like no other voice you would ever hear, it seemed such a deliberate effort – launched into a 'topic' before the man had even sat down. It amused and amazed as much as it intimidated. He asserted himself just by making his stage entrance onto what Thoreau, walking down here from Province-town in all weathers, had in awe called 'the great beach'.

The ocean rolled and thundered. The sand shone. The cliffs of stark dunes overhead, green grass and tiny twisted shrub pine against the gold sand, gleamed with wild rose bushes. Our happiest times were here, at the edge of the land, the ocean, the dunes. Beyond 'Joan's beach', where a wartime army hut had been moved as a summer cottage for a lady from New York and her painter boyfriend, still stretched the outermost Cape, forever humming in your ears from the ocean, the emptiness of that long wild ocean beach where you could still contentedly walk, make love and skinny dip.

But 'Joan's beach' was a riot. The great beach was replaced every afternoon by the great society. Each year Joan's weathered old beach hut sank more abjectly into the sand while around it rose the mercilessly stylized *avant-garde* house of a wealthy Leninist from Philadelphia. A leathery old man with a shaven head and showing off a powerful chest, a man who looked just as photographically virile as the old Picasso, walked with too emphatic strides to the 'nudies' beach. In the great clown tradition of the good old American summertime, pliant young girls in striped tank suits and Huck Finn country straw hats sat in the lotus position practicing Yoga. The ocean gamboled, young men dived into rollers and then hopped up and down in the water waiting for a wave to float them back to shore. Down the beach couples lay about open, free and friendly as if they had just made the happiest love. Red Japanese kites with long tails bobbed up and down as if wheeled by the screams of the children on the cliffs.

In the midst of all this Edmund Wilson was hoarsely at the center of everyone's attention, sometimes forced against his will into the usual gossip and polemic. He sat without ease, he scooped up a handful of sand and let it drift slowly through his half-clenched fist as people jumping out of the water gathered around him only to jump back into the water. So many staring, giggling and deadly scrutinizers, guessing that he was 'someone', made him nervous, but he unhappily sat on, unable to make his escape. So he talked. He talked as if reluctant to talk but was too stubborn to stop. He talked as if talking was a physical difficulty forced upon him by a disagreeable world. But it was one he had learned to use for his own purposes, and even with cunning in short, shy, killing observations. Then, looking as if he had heard himself for the first time, he would throw his head back in a loud whinnying laugh.

He talked about what he was reading and writing. He talked as he wrote, from current preoccupations only. His talk was as formal as his writing. He invariably led off with a topic. He had been reading this new thing of Sartre's, and had to say that the fellow was not as big a windbag as he had been led to believe. He liked the man's big French radical schemes. This Allegro man and his brazen but not uninteresting guesses on the mysterious particles and practices of the Essenes. An irritable rejoinder to Gilbert Seldes, who had been telling a story about getting tight with T. S. Eliot in the twenties. Gilbert had the date wrong. A new book about our animal aggressive tradition. Everything the new young anthropologists were telling him he had known from Darwin. He was still a nineteenth-century mechanist and materialist: 'We must simply get along without religion.' As for T. S. Eliot, he had the story in his notebook *and* the exact date. Had you by any chance looked into Swinburne's novels? The amusing structure of the Hungarian language, which he was just then learning? 'My dear boy,' he had greeted me on the beach the week before, 'have I yet given you my lecture on Hungarian? No? Sit down and please listen.' There was also this new book on magic. He was very proud of his magician's lore and often set out to do tricks that did not always succeed. He was too distracted. At my little daughter's birthday party one summer he came with his equipment and disappeared into the lean-to for newspapers he said he needed for his act. Time passed, no Edmund. We looked in and found him absorbedly reading the newspapers.

Everything alive to him was alive as words, had to find its exact finicky representation in every single trace of his experience and of his reading. Much of the day and often late into the night he sat in his great big study in the rambling old house just off Route 6. He sat there with the stuffed owl that he hated, with the sets of Scott and Dickens that had come down to him from Wilsons and Kimballs and Mathers like the gold-topped cane and the family pictures he could never stop studying. Just outside the study was the great set of the Latin and Greek classics in their heavy striped bindings. Inside the study were the books he used for each book, like the many-volumed Michelet he had needed for *To The Finland Station.*

There were several desks in that study, and he moved from one to the other as he worked now on one book, now on another. He wrote always by hand, in his elegant and peremptory script, and there were as many projects going on at once in that study as in a Renaissance painter's atelier. Everything in the household revolved around his day's work and the regimen needed to accomplish it. He had his own record player in that room, his own bathroom just a few steps down from his study, his own bedroom when he wanted it in this separate suite of rooms. Out on Route 6 cars screeched on their way to and from Provincetown the pleasure place, girls with streaming hair bicycled past in halters and shorts. But inside the

study that was deep inside the house off the main highway, Edmund
Wilson protected by his tall beautiful European wife Elena sat
writing at one desk or another, reading in one language or another,
eagerly waiting for Elena to bring the mail back so that he could
get still more reading matter and letters to answer.

He lived to read and write. Each new language after the Latin
and Greek, French and Italian, he had learned at school, the Russian,
German and Hebrew he had acquired mostly by himself, the
Hungarian he was now so proud of, the Yiddish he typically
attempted from grammars after he had learned the Hebrew
alphabet, was a 'love affair', he once said to me, with some subtle
new syntax to love. He laughed at academic specialists with
their proprietary talk of 'my field', more usually in modern
American 'my area'. One of his favorite antagonists was a scholar
who was always pressing him to read Cervantes (Spanish for
some reason never interested him). 'Elena and I have been
attempting Don Quixote,' he once calculatedly told the famous
prof. 'and I have to admit that we find it just a mite dull.'
The prof. 'turned pale and stood up shaking. "*Harvard* thinks
differently"!'

Yet what Wilson wrote dealt so much with the plight of personality, his fascination with his own family, his need to involve
himself with other people, that one could see even in his every
sentence the extraordinary effort he put out, by words alone, to
free himself from bookish solitude. Life was one elaborately
constructed sentence after another, and he had been sentenced to
the sentence.

The formality of sentence structure even on the beach, like the
aloofness of his manner even when you were drinking and gossiping
with him in his own house, was like nothing any of us would ever
see again. Ponderously shy, abrupt, exact and exacting, he was
matter-of-fact in a style of old-fashioned American hardness. He
could be massive, unyielding on the smallest matters. Why did I
always feel that I had to shout in order to reach him? There was
that famous distraction, the great bald dome thinking away,
arranging its sentences, even as he talked to you. But of course he
made no easy splash of talk to swim in, as the rest of us did at the

17

many cocktail parties. To depart from the question he had set was to find yourself addressing questions to the air.

He was tyrannically correct with himself and officiously correct about everybody else. The correct word, the unquestionable historical detail, was a professional matter. Competence was the only right relation to others. He worked from fragments and études in his notebook; short flights were the natural span of his intellectual imagination. But he had also absorbed from his passion for grammar (and no doubt his long solitude; he was an only child with a deaf mother and a neurasthenic father) some unAmerican patience and thoroughness. He knew nothing else so well as how to make a book. He made books out of his intellectual satires against intellectuals, out of the light verse he sent his friends at Christmas, out of his *New Yorker* book reviews, out of his hatred of Robert Moses's high-handed urban renewal, out of his compassion for Indians, out of his typical belief (based on early holidays there) that Canada represented a better, uncorrupted, version of his own too big and too powerful country, out of his aversion to the endless bookkeeping forced on American taxpayers by the Internal Revenue Service. This somehow turned into a book against the Cold War.

Wilson made books out of virtually everything that crossed his mind. But certain subjects (especially American, nineteenth-century, related to the Civil War and the Gilded Age) never just *crossed* that mind. They stayed there, decade after decade, to be used as articles after they had first been sketched in his notebook-journal. Then they got re-written for his books and would be rewritten again for new editions of these books. What he knew, he knew; what he read he remembered; what he had seen of San Diego or Jerusalem or Odessa stayed with him forever. No one else I knew had so much patience with his own writing, his own impressions, the stories he told and retold from notebook to article to book to the next meeting in his living room. He could recast his own writing – and yours – with the same air of easily inhabiting the world by words alone. No one else I knew had the same impulse to correct and rewrite everybody else. He once returned from lunch to the *New Yorker*, saw on someone else's table a proof of my review of

The Shores of Light, and calmly changed a date in it. After reading a book in bed, 'I often rewrite it in my sleep'.

He could be hilarious in the retentiveness, the obstinacy, his intense personal relation to any book or subject that he liked very much or disliked very much. Discussing *The Scarlet Letter*, a book that as a literary modernist he easily disliked because it belonged to the old American schoolroom or too much to his own past (on his mother's side he was descended from the Puritan hierarchs, the Mathers), he was angrily asked by a young professor of 'American Studies' – 'May I ask when you last read the book?' '1915', Wilson said breezily.

Later, relaxed on the beach after the great crowd had gone to a cocktail party at a psychohistorian's (it was to begin as a memorial service on the anniversary of Hiroshima, and one could see trailing up from the beach a procession of shoeless intellectuals, the ladies in chic white outfits, carrying candles), Wilson was rosy with Scotch and full of his special belief in conspiracies. In the total jeremiad against the American state he was to write as preface to his wonderful book on the Civil War, *Patriotic Gore*, Wilson blithely accepted the historian Charles A. Beard's dark suggestion that Pearl Harbor was somehow fostered by F.D.R. himself '. . . it has been argued, to me quite convincingly, that this act was foreseen by our government and – in order to make our antagonists strike the first blow – deliberately not forestalled at a time when a Japanese delegation was attempting to negotiate peace'. Now, getting liberated as crowd, bottle and day dwindled, he said with the caustic smile he reserved for anxiously Americanized and patriotic Jewish intellectuals – 'Bobby Kennedy knows who *really* killed his brother – and is not telling.' 'Edmund, you're going overboard the way you did in that preface!' He leaned back on a sandhill with perfect confidence, 'My dear boy, you mustn't discount my legal background.'

'My legal background'! He meant Edmund Wilson Sr., one of the best lawyers of his day in New Jersey, at one time attorney-general of the State and, though a Republican, invited by Woodrow Wilson to join his cabinet in 1913. Edmund Jr. seemed to trace his own ties, quirks and obsessions to his father, who was a passionate

admirer of Lincoln the lawyer (the tragedy of Lincoln runs through
Patriotic Gore as the tragedy of the superior man in America). The
father identified with Lincoln the melancholic. Though a lawyer
for the Pennsylvania Railroad and able to give his less finicky
relatives advice about the stock market, Wilson Sr. would not buy a
share of stock. He regarded such transactions as a form of gambling.
Like many brilliant men of his generation, he regarded his own life
as forfeit to the big-business spirit in America. He became a 'nervous
invalid', a total hypochondriac; his professional career yielded to
his concern with his own symptoms. His mother, a heartier type,
not 'intellectual', went deaf under the strain of her husband's
breakdown.

Edmund Wilson knew he was 'odd', and was always looking into
his ancestry for the sources of his own obsessions as well as the
intellectual interests plainly derived from the many preachers,
lawyers, doctors behind him. When I was briefly a professor at
Amherst, he suddenly dropped in on me – by taxi all the way from
Wellfleet – and wanted to look up the college records of his grandfather, Thaddeus Wilson D. D., a Presbyterian minister whose old
Hebrew grammar he now used himself. He wrote about his parents
and grandparents – 'The fact was that I knew almost nobody else.
I knew they had their doubts about me, and that in order to prove
myself I should have to show that a writer could become a successful
professional.' T. S. Matthews, who had known Wilson on the *New
Republic*, liked to say that Wilson's parents had once bought him a
baseball suit – but that he had gone on reading even after he had
put on the suit. As a writer he had indeed 'proved' himself thirty
years before, with *Axel's Castle*. But, despite his many books since
and his long record of production, he had become with increasing
insistence a kind of self-proclaimed outsider to the 'America I see
depicted in *Life* magazine'. He liked in the 1960s to say, in the
sight of so many 'sophisticated' academicians, that 'old fogeyism'
was creeping in. He now made a point of stating – boasting of? –
how little money he had accumulated. Thanks to his worrisome
income-tax case, he was in financial trouble virtually to the very
end of his life in 1972. *The Cold War and the Income Tax* was
however a bit of political afterthought after he was nailed by the

government for neglecting to pay his taxes. The truth seems to be that he was too distracted even to sign the returns that his wife prepared for them. But when the government attached much of his income and fined him severely, it became a point of defiance with him, as against the swollen crazily prosperous sixties, *not* to have amassed much money and to be, in the good old American style, 'agin the government'. My friend Peter Shaw wrote that in the sixties every typical product of America (including the student rebellion) 'lacked modesty of scale'. Edmund Wilson was certainly not 'modest'; but he did enjoy being out of scale with the rest of the country.

At several periods in his life, he noted in his journal, he had felt impelled to write protests against various officials of the United States government; he first wrote one as a sergeant in the A.E.F. Medical Corps! As if he were one of his own forebears, he now lived in two 'old-fashioned country towns', Wellfleet, Mass., and Talcottville, New York; he depended on a small income from one of his few relatives who had gone into business; he did not drive a car or use a typewriter; he did not teach, give lectures, join honorary societies that asked to honor him. When he at last accepted the Emerson–Thoreau medal of the American Academy of Arts and Sciences, he explained that he must refuse to make a speech and insisted on reading his translation of Pushkin's *The Bronze Horseman*. When he accepted the MacDowell medal, he terrified the chairman by rolling the medal between his palms to show that he could make it disappear.

He would not play the game. Every year he became ceremonially more difficult, seemingly more perverse, more alienated from what President Johnson blissfully called 'the great society', from the endless American sociability, from the 'successful career' that American writers strive for as thirstily as professors and oil executives. Of course he had authority, and how proudly he could use it. To ward off the many people who want something from a 'name', he had a postcard printed up on which it was noted (with a check against the appropriate box) that Edmund Wilson does not read manuscripts for strangers; does not write articles or books to order; does not write forewords or introductions; does not make statements for publicity purposes; does not do any kind of editorial work, judge literary contests, give interviews, broadcast or appear on television; does not answer questionnaires, contribute to or take part in symposiums. And so on!

As the contrast deepened each year between Wilson and the America 'I see depicted in *Life* magazine', his concern with right words and standards seemed to become more intense, his irritation with sloppiness and misuse even more pronounced, his sense of his own intellectual honor loftier and yet more anguished. The old radical was becoming the old curmudgeon.

Behind Wilson's ever more pressing urge to make order of his life by words, behind the obsessive journal-keeper feeding on the one book he never had to give up writing – a day as its own subject, its only expressive task – there was some patrician belief that through style everything, even in his disordered country, would yet fall into place. He had always been a fussy corrector of everything he read. Now the authority derived from his sound education, from his many books and almost 'bewildering' interests, from being *Edmund Wilson*, became as necessary as the articulation of the bones to the movement of the body. This insistence on 'correctness' – as of a judge or minister or national leader in the days when a few solitary geniuses molded American culture – became basic to the sense of his role in American life. Let the young and the newer stocks have their pretentious social science theories and academic careers and ridiculous 'new criticism'; he was the last American man of letters, the great anachronism – and not without mischief.

Wilson now depended on 'style' in an aristocratic–political sense more familiar to English universities and the House of Commons than to American intellectuals. He seemed to read the young writers with more attention than they read themselves, and loved to point out to a writer his misuse of a word and some error in detail. 'Trotsky was killed not with a pickax but with an ice ax. You made the same mistake in your last book.' Sometimes the pressure to write well was so grinding that, as one noticed when the notebooks began to come out, there was not a picture seen but just the effort to make one. Writers his too concrete mind could not grasp – Blake,

Kafka – he dismissed with a wave of his hand. What he understood he understood.

There was a kind of political majesty to all this. Behind the pressing personal urge to correctness, I saw the moral significance of 'right words' to Wilson's class – the professional gentry of lawyers, preachers, educators, scientists, which from the time of New England's clerical oligarchs had remained the sustaining class of American intellectual life. Despite all these eager beavers from the 'newer' stocks, the few figures with the most unquestioned influence still represented – and often in the person of Edmund Wilson himself – the old American clerisy. These were still the policy makers, where silly imitative 'new critics' spoke haughtily of 'irrelevant texture' in Shakespeare. Was the intellect in America to be banished to the new mass universities? The true thinkers were the policy makers behind the scenes who, no matter how many billions heaped up by the old robber barons they gave out as heads of the great foundations, were as detached as Henry Adams from the oily propaganda of American business.

Wilson thus seemed the one man of letters in the American tradition who still represented the traditional American caste of professional diplomats like George Kennan, judges like Oliver Wendell Holmes and Learned Hand, scholars who were lawgivers like Noah Webster. No wonder that *Patriotic Gore*, our American Plutarch, ended on Justice Holmes, as it began with Harriet Beecher Stowe and that most superior intellect, Abraham Lincoln. Such men and women were 'the capable', as Sinclair Lewis (a doctor's son) had admiringly called the lonely doctors, philosophic lawyers and scientists who in his work resist the bitch goddess that William James (another doctor) had called American success. Though business ruled the roost and money was more important to everybody, it was 'the capable', who came from a long tradition of professional concern, who still kept up for others the standards Edmund Wilson grew up with.

The chief expression all this took was the bitter polemical preface he wrote in 1962 to the long-delayed *Patriotic Gore*. It had taken him fifteen years to put the book together from a lifetime of reading and absorption in the literature of the Civil War. In the summer of 1962 his bitterness against the American state took the form of a preface that was really an effort to deny the love of the American past and his belief in American moral heroism that made the book itself so moving.

Like so much else in his work, *Patriotic Gore* also took off from family history. One of his earliest memories seems to have been seeing the original two-volume set of General Grant's memoirs, published by Mark Twain (and sold by subscription to all good Americans) as a service to the strange man who had crushed the South but had proved a disaster as president both to the nation and to himself. After he left the White House, he went bankrupt, was cheated of his own money and, dying of throat cancer, undertook the Memoirs at Mark Twain's urging in order to provide for his family.

Wilson, so deep in 'all that Civil War stuff' that the enchanted reader could not help following him at every turn of the great narrative, nevertheless opened the book with a preface that read as if it had been composed to drive off anyone who might still have the illusion that the Civil War was historically necessary. As if the title (from *Maryland My Maryland*) were not surly and sarcastic enough, Wilson compared the Northern 'refusal to grant the South its independence' (certainly an unhistorical way of putting it) to the Soviet suppression in 1956 of the Hungarian revolt. The history of the United States was nothing but a big-power drive. The United States had been an aggressor against the Indians, against the Mexicans, against the South. 'The institution of slavery, which the Northern states had by this time got rid of, thus supplied the militant Union North with the rabble-rousing moral issue which is necessary in every modern war to make the conflict appear as a melodrama . . . The north's determination to preserve the Union was simply the form that the power drive now took.'

'I am trying', Wilson claimed, 'to remove the whole subject from the plane of morality and to give an objective account of the expansion of the United States.' This was hardly Wilson's forte. The value of his book of course lay in its intense biographical method. Wilson was no more at ease in 'objective' history than he was in removing any subject 'from the plane of morality'. His main text, so assiduous in tracing every detail of character and intelligence in his main figures, was full of the most obvious gratitude for what they had contributed to the eradication of slavery and the preservation of the country. But on and on Wilson went in his preface, ticking off Pearl Harbor as Roosevelt's doing, ticking off Hiroshima, ticking off our postwar belligerence toward Russia, ticking off our preparations for bacteriological and biological warfare. The United States, it seemed, had obstructed Castro's socialist revolution, thus forcing him to seek support from the Communists. (Castro was himself to give the lie to this in acknowledging his long Communist background.) But Wilson was in such a state about any and all wars fought by the United States that he was wild enough to write that, though Jews had strong reasons for fighting Hitler, it was wrong of them to support the war, since 'the extermination of six million Jews was already very far advanced by the time the United States took action'.

Wilson then excused the Southern resistance to the civil rights movement on the grounds that Southerners 'have never entirely recognized the authority of the Washington government'. This was as mistaken in fact as it was foolish in theory. The South was the most militaristic section of the country and had been enthusiastic for war against Spain in 1898, against Germany in 1917, in Korea in 1950. Southerners in the 1840s had led the attack against Mexico and had wanted to annex Cuba. Lincoln had said over and over what the North knew to be the simple truth – it was the South's attempt to foist the slave system on the free territories that led to the Civil War.

Wilson's bitterness on the subject of America's 'power-drive' of course represented the despair of many Americans as their government vainly attempted to 'contain' the whole world against Communism. The government since 1941 had become too autonomous and powerful. But Wilson, very much like Thoreau in his own passionate political essays against the American state, made no effort to prove his case; he just helped himself out with terrific images taken from his reading in the power drives of animals. There was little in that preface one could deal with as historical evidence. It was a series of defiant assertions in the old American style: government is not to be trusted. Many younger Americans were soon to feel this, but they had radical solutions for still *more* government, Leninist style, that Wilson laughed at.

A question naturally emerged. Why, if Wilson felt that way about the Civil War and about American history in general, should he want to spend fifteen years on the book? To which the only possible answer was another question. Why, if he said he felt that way about the Civil War, should he have written such an extraordinary book around it?

For *Patriotic Gore* is really a great book. It was not only the greatest single performance of Wilson's unique career as a man of letters (and contained in passing the most profound considerations on literature in America I had ever read). It made the passion that went into the war, and into the disillusion that followed it, more affecting than any other contemporary book on this greatest of national American experiences. It had in particular a fullness of historical atmosphere, a sensitivity to the great personages, of the vital writers and leaders, that made the reader see Mrs. Stowe, Lincoln, Grant, Sherman and the others as commanding figures in a great American epic. Though Abraham Lincoln 'examined the mechanical devices that were brought to him in the years of his Presidency and is reported to have understood them, he does not seem to have been much impressed by the development of machinery in America or even much interested in it'. 'Grant, dying of cancer of the throat and writing his Personal Memoirs to provide for his impoverished family, dictated the book until it became impossible to use his voice. Humiliated, bankrupt and voiceless, on the very threshold of death, sleepless at night sitting up in a chair as if he were still in the field and could not risk losing touch with developments, he relived his old campaigns.'

There, in the heroes, the writers, the sensitive consciences, the faithful diarists of the conflict, was Edmund Wilson's own story. There was no real social history in this book of studies in the literature of the Civil War, no grasp of the real social issues and movements behind the war and nineteenth-century America. History to the 'old radical' was still, as it had been to Emerson, biography.

As the sixties darkened into war, and he became increasingly ill, his sense of himself, of his necessary authority, became more pronounced and more tragic. At a party in Ed O'Connor's house in the Wellfleet woods, Wilson drunk and defiant said laughingly that the F.B.I. would be suspicious of him. 'I've been married four times!' As he stumbled out of the party and down the stairs, the consort of the famous historian who was so proud of knowing exactly who was who on *la plage des intellectuels* said throatily: 'Really, shouldn't someone look after the poor old man?'

He was lonely in Wellfleet all the year round, and he was afraid of dying. He gave me the magnificently desolate Audubon print of two long-haired squirrels, each alone on its branch of a tree and looking as apprehensive as only a squirrel can look even when it has cornered some food against the evening. He could not stand those squirrels any longer. They reminded him too much of himself. Death was the antagonist that his obstinately old-fashioned materialistic philosophy could not defeat. It could give him no help. His grandfather's old Presbyterianism was no help. Was it possible that Jews had an answer? The question was as delightful to me as Edmund's once writing that he had lost himself in five thousand years of Jewish history and could not get out. One of his favorite maxims in his lonely Wellfleet winters was the plea *Hazak Hazak Vinithazak* addressed by orthodox Jews in synagogue as they finish reading each scriptural book. *Be strong. Be strong, and let us strengthen one another.* In Hebrew letters, this is engraven on his tombstone in the Wellfleet cemetery.

ANGUS WILSON

❧

Edmund Wilson

In my whole career in writing, nothing has been so important to me as the encouragement that Edmund Wilson gave me. When, in 1950, I read his review of my first book, *The Wrong Set*, it affected me in quite a different way from all the others. I had been lucky with the large attention I got for these stories. Some of the critics were people whose praise I was proud to receive. But Edmund Wilson was somebody quite different. His work was part of my life before I had ever thought of writing. Three of his books had affected me deeply at different times and in very different areas of my life. To receive his praise for my first book and to continue to receive his encouragements and warning counsels was, not as with other critics to hear voices more or less meaningful from outside, but to listen to an oracle from somewhere deep inside myself.

When I was at Oxford, like many another young man I enjoyed myself greatly by reading, at random, books quite outside the history syllabus which was my chosen study – not, I must say, to the improvement of my final degree. It was then that, freed from earlier constraints which arose from wondering whether literature should be my university study, I read most of the great 'modern' novels of this century and really delighted in them in a headless, carefree way that I can never recapture. In one single long vacation I devoured *A la Recherche du temps perdu* and *Ulysses*. But a curious mind, especially one trained to historical studies, does seek to impose some shape and order upon his most scattered delights. It was in my second year that the man who had rooms next door to me in college – a Byronic aesthete with an eye for good things –

gave me Edmund's *Axel's Castle* with the suggestion that it might clear up a lot of the muddle which my chatter suggested was rattling around in my head. He was quite right. The book was a treasure trove. Its clear argument in pleasing, vigorous English cut a way through my muddled delights that gave them a much fuller pleasure in some order. I should not now accept his treatment of Naturalism, or, at any rate, his treatment of Zola. We had one or two most fruitful arguments about the Rougon–Macquart novels in which, with his characteristic skirmishing manner of verbal warfare, he often succeeded in penetrating my battle lines at the very moment when I thought he was in full retreat. But, Zola's basic romanticism apart, *Axel's Castle* connected for me then the Romantic world, whose contours, even though no literature student, I knew reasonably well, with Proust and Joyce, whose monstrous shapes perplexed and alarmed as much as they delighted me. The book made me at home with two giants whose works began to fertilize my imagination then in a way that was to enrich my whole life and, I think, my books when I later came to write. *Axel's Castle* led me on to Eliot and to Valéry at a time when I had ceased to read poetry, finding the 'modern' idiom repellent in a way that I did not in novels. I think that, over and above the clear cogent argument and style, two characteristic virtues of Edmund's work particularly made me captive. The first was his capacity – even with great monstrous chronicles like those of Marcel in pursuit of the madeleine's clue and of Bloom's wandering day in Dublin – to give outlines of the books he was discussing – something I believe most essential to good criticism – without desiccating the recounted narratives and without divorcing them from the body of his argument. I know of no other critic of novels who has done this so successfully. Secondly, in his chapter on Valéry, he recounts the poet's arrogant and contemptuous treatment of Anatole France in his speech to the Academy when he came to occupy France's vacant chair. Now I had read and loved Anatole France as a young adolescent. By my Oxford time, I was aware of his deficiencies, but I was also aware that my defensive feeling for him was not wholly a sentimentalism. Edmund in that chapter did what, I think, only he could do. He very lightly castigated Valéry

29

for the impiety of his speech, he made amends for it to Anatole France without exaggerating his worth, and he did all this without suggesting that the incident affected the high quality of Valéry's own work. Fairness, tact (something not usually attributed to him), relative values that were strongly enough felt to allow for moderation and consideration of the good in the second rate – these are rare qualities in literary critics, as I have learnt since I forsook the study of history as my main pursuit for the study of literature. But I know that had Edmund Wilson's treatment of France in discussing Valéry (or, for that matter, his treatment of Shaw, another of my adolescent idols, in discussing Yeats) been as dismissive and dogmatic as that of so many academic critics, whom I was not to know for many years to come, I should have turned away from the whole subject with disgust.

The next great impact of Edmund's work came to me as I made my way in cold and slow trains (often delayed by time bombs) from Bishop's Stortford to Liverpool Street and back again in the last weeks of my wartime work at the British Museum before joining the Intelligence Service. There was time for many books then. I remember vividly, in improbable juxtaposition Keats's letters and *Aurora Leigh* and Diderot's *La Religieuse*. But the book that shook me and then helped me to reassemble my shaken frame was *To the Finland Station*. I had been, like all my generation (or all that had any intelligent apprehensions), intensely 'politically conscious' in the years from 1935 or 1936 until after the invasion of Prague, when I concluded that happy life, if not life itself was imminently threatened and gave up the last months of peace to 'personal life'. Such were the terms – 'political consciousness' and 'personal life' in contrast – in which I thought in those years of highly justified, yet modish and muddled left-wing activity. It was not only events that had brought me to this United Front, near Fellow Travelling attitude which I shared with many of my generation, but the history teaching (even of right- wing historians) of my time at Oxford which was always deterministic. Once again, a book of Edmund's proved cathartic, for it approached the Russian Revolution and its Marxist source through a whole discussion of historical method going back to Vico. My deeply entrenched views, shaken though they had been by reports of Communist behaviour in Catalonia and by the Russo–German pact, would (perhaps because of my doubts) have refused any frontal attack; but a sympathetic yet totally effective unpicking of the complicated tapestry of historical determinism on which my views rested did much to change my whole outlook. I felt (and I was largely right) that Edmund Wilson had travelled the same road that I had, but that he had the power to light up the seams and crevasses that I had only glimpsed. He made me sure that I had been right always to resist any suggestion of 'joining the party'. It was a turning point in my life. Any violent frontal attack, anything suggesting the hysteria which has always repelled me in Orwell would have sent me in the opposite direction. I am deeply grateful to Wilson for this. And, incidentally, I know of no more exciting piece of historical narration than his account of the journey of Lenin and Krupskaya to Petrograd that ends the book.

Somewhat later in the war, when in the long black-out evenings of my billet life during my Intelligence work at Bletchley I read and read, I came upon the third contribution of Edmund Wilson to my intellectual growth. I don't say that it was the most important but it was certainly, at the time, the most surprising. Of all the authors that had eaten into my bones from childhood, Dickens was the most important to me. I was aware always as I read and re-read his novels of the endless layers of meanings (I think I should have called them dreams then) that existed for me in his work. I was always vaguely aware that this was not the view taken by the more serious literary critics of the day. I did not read academic literary criticism until after I became a writer. But I had read disparaging essays about him by Aldous Huxley and Virginia Woolf; I had seen E. M. Forster's contemptuous view of him in print. And now here was Edmund Wilson putting into words so much that I felt about the novelist I cared for most. What was more, the next essay in *The Wound and the Bow* concerned Kipling, an author whose pull upon me was as early and tenacious if somewhat more ambiguous than that of Dickens. And once again Edmund Wilson had much to say about the fundamental seriousness of a writer whom I knew to be dismissed by most clever people. I have written a book on Charles Dickens since then and I am in the course of writing one on Rudyard Kipling: I should now say that a little of what Edmund said about Dickens was misconceived and that he neglected a very important part of Kipling's work. But that is not important. At a time when other clever people simply neglected these two great writers, he had the independence of mind, the good sense, the eye for their importance and the humility to assess them without prejudice and see how good they were. And to say it loudly. Had I not found his serious criticism of these two authors whom I knew instinctively to be good, I should, I am sure, have turned away from any other literary critics, however interesting, who disparaged them, with disgust; but, with Edmund Wilson's backing, I felt free to read the other critics with interest and yet disregard their blind failure to appreciate the unfashionable great.

And this openness was, indeed, to strike me as the most agreeable of all Edmund's delightful facets when I came to meet him. We met at long intervals over years, but he would always greet me with – 'I've been reading some of Hugh Walpole lately – um – um – well there's something there, not probably a lot, but something. I must read some more. What do you think, um?' Or, 'James Branch Cabell now. I wonder. I don't think so. But we must see. I'll read. You read. Write to me. Let me know, um.' But he was *truly* open, not just to the unfashionable, but to a new view of the modish – Dujna Barnes, or my own short stories when they first came out and 'were all the rage'. He thought always for himself and he was omnivorous.

We first met, when in 1960, on a first wonderful dreamlike tour of the United States, beginning at Los Angeles, I reached Cambridge, Mass., to lecture at Harvard. He had booked a room for me and my friend at a small hotel and we then went to dine with him and Elena. Their courteous friendliness and hospitality were more than I'd ever anticipated – and Edmund's solicitude about the hotel was touching. We spent a long, gently boozy, talkative and delightful evening, in which, as I remember, although he was a most argumentative man, he genuinely seemed to consider everything I had to say about the States, about which I was brimming

over, although it all must have been weirdly naive. Indeed he was
the only New Englander or New Yorker who heard with patience,
though not without doubts, my paeans of praise of Los Angeles
with which I had fallen in love. He seemed to me then proteanly
to vary from moment to moment, from squire to radical, to
radical squire, to journalist, to man-about-town, to don, to book-
loving child, but it was, of course, as I came to see in my later
meetings with him, that he was a unique personality. In that first
meeting I was trying to place him in a category and he would not
be so placed but ran off into another category until at last I ceased
to try to pin him down and accepted him for somebody I had
never met before.

After that I met him a number of times at the Basil Hotel on his
London visits. Once more a splendid host but somehow implying
that he could offer me in London not the delights of civilization but
only the delights of a place that had fallen into decadence or relapsed
into barbarism, but, of course, as I was a native, I should no doubt
be used to . . . But when I refused to accept this version of the very
simple service offered by the Basil Hotel, he dropped all that and
became himself, for, in fact, he enjoyed England, and his love–hate
of which I'd heard so much from those who met him here at the time
of *Europe Without Baedeker*, was in fact a love–irritation, no more.
Only once did I ever see him disconcerted, and that was when I
arrived at the Basil Hotel, expecting Elena to be there, with a large
bunch of white tulips, to find Edmund on his own. Some teasing
quality in me led me to present him with the flowers in homage
to himself. I have seldom seen a man so embarrassed. He accepted
them with many ums, held them behind his back, reversed uneasily
into the bedroom, got rid of them, and returned to the private
sitting room as though such an unbelievable thing as tulips presented
by a man to a man had never existed. He immediately began to
talk fascinatingly about Gosse, for nothing, I think, so delighted,
so set him at ease as the more dubious aspects of the life of men of
letters. I told him of my experience of the Wise forgeries when, as
an assistant in the British Museum Library, I saw them added to the
national collection. Engrossed in the psychology of Wise's play
upon Gosse's vanity, we went down to the dining room, far too

delighted, he to half apologize for the British food, I to state its superiority for discerning palates.

It was at that time that he told me of his reading aloud my novels to his wife. I cannot say what pleasure this news gave to me. In some part, because it was what I have always liked to think readers might do but supposed no longer happened. But more so because I instantly realized that, although it was highly unlikely that he would successfully imitate my characters' speech or indeed attempt to, he would somehow get the book 'right' in his overall reading. But I like most to remember his almost shy piety and grave pleasure, when, visiting us where we live in Suffolk, we took him to the nearby villages of Rattlesden and Buxhall, there in the churchyards to find tombstones of members of his mother's family, the Kimballs, who had left England for New England in the seventeenth century. He was surely in his radicalism the most tradition-loving of men, a New England squire, so acutely concerned for anyone who might have been harmed by the tradition which had made him, that he found it necessary to investigate in turn, the cause of the South, the American Indians, and Canada. He was a most bellicose, gentle, and chivalrous man.

BETTE CROUSE MELE

Edmund Wilson and the Iroquois

In 1960 I began a correspondence with Edmund Wilson after reading his articles in the *New Yorker* magazine about the New York State Iroquois. I am a Seneca woman, born at the Allegany Seneca Reservation in western New York State. Mr. Wilson had visited the Seneca at Allegany in 1958 with Dr. William Fenton, a noted anthropologist, who is a widely recognized authority on the Iroquois. I had written to Mr. Wilson because his articles, which became the book *Apologies to the Iroquois*, had greatly impressed me and I was hopeful that he would meet me. Mr. Wilson usually did not answer letters or grant interviews and responded to these requests with a card stating that he did not do so, but my letter had interested him.

When my letter to Edmund Wilson arrived in Talcottville, forwarded by the *New Yorker*, Dr. Fenton was visiting Wilson and advised him that he did indeed know me. As a young man beginning his field work he had camped beside the house of my late great-uncle, Jonas Snow, brother of my grandmother. My grandmother later adopted Dr. Fenton into the Seneca Hawk clan. Dr. Fenton had given valuable assistance to Mr. Wilson when Wilson was collecting material for his articles on the Iroquois, even providing him with entrée to secret rituals that are closed to non-Indians. Mr. Wilson was concerned about the effect of his writing about these ceremonies of the Seneca. He was anxious that it would not be well received and be considered a betrayal of their trust.

Mr. Wilson responded to my letter by inviting me to any of his three residences at Cambridge, Wellfleet or Talcottville. Two years later, after sporadic correspondence, I went to visit Mr.

Wilson in his beloved stone house in Talcottville. My greatest fear of meeting Wilson was that I would not know how to talk to him. When I had written him I stated that I had been greatly impressed by the amount of research he had done on the Iroquois. He was interested to discuss my reaction to his book as he had not been able to gauge the reaction of the Iroquois to it. Conversation came easily and I spent a comfortable afternoon relating to him the reasons that I had so much appreciated *Apologies*, beginning with the fact of his sensitive portrayal of each Iroquois that he encountered. He was delighted that I had recognized the people at Allegany that he had described but not named.

Apologies to the Iroquois presented us with dignity and intelligence as contemporary people in conflict with the value system of the dominant society. It removed us from the archives and attics of anthropology and archaeology and portrayed us as a viable cultural group.

For many years the Quakers of the Philadelphia Friends' Yearly Meeting had helped the Senecas oppose the Kinzua Dam Project, a 'flood control' project of the Army Corps of Engineers that would take 10,000 acres of the Allegany Reservation. The Senecas at Allegany should have been protected by the Pickering Treaty of 1794 which guaranteed to us our lands, stating in Article III 'and the United States will never claim the same, nor disturb the SENECA nation, nor any of the Six Nations, or of their Indian friends residing thereon and united with them, in the free use and enjoyment thereof: but it shall remain theirs, until they choose to sell the same to the people of the United States, who have the right to purchase'. The Seneca clearly did not choose to sell and the Quakers were incensed at the intention of the U.S. Congress to break the oldest, unabrogated Indian treaty.

Dwight D. Eisenhower, as President of the U.S., had twice refused to sign the appropriations bill for construction of the dam and Mr. Wilson was hopeful that we would retain our land, land that had never been occupied by any but Seneca people and their aboriginal forebears. But we were unable to get wide public support for our opposition to the dam; due to a peculiar syndrome that exists in eastern U.S., the general public is ignorant of Indians east of the Mississippi and this problem was a great handicap for us. Eventually President John Kennedy refused to impound the funds appropriated for the dam by Congress as he had 'concluded that it is not possible to halt the construction of the Kinzua Dam'. This latter event took place after publication of *Apologies* and distressed Mr. Wilson considerably.

Edmund Wilson understood the difficulties I had in relating to the non-Indian community in which I lived at the time of the publication of the Iroquois articles. My problems are a result of growing up in western New York communities, which I consider prejudiced against Indians, especially in areas adjacent to reservations. Indians, as a result of prejudice exercised toward them by the dominant culture and reinforced by texts used in the educational system, frequently develop poor self-esteem and a good deal of resentment. It is also difficult for us to read much of the history of Indian affairs in the U.S. without feeling a great deal of anguish, as most of it is slanted toward justifying the outrages practised against Indians in the pursuit of trade, settlement, and colonization. Almost without exception historical materials refer to Indians as savage, barbaric and primitive.

As a child I lived with my family off the reservation for about six years in a community where we were the only Indian family. My parents sent me to a private school where they hoped I would be spared the bullying of the rougher element at public schools, but I was sometimes subjected to stoning or attacks with iced snow balls as well as verbal abuse. My father was frequently referred to as 'chief' in a most derogatory fashion, my brothers were also called 'chief' in a like fashion and I was called 'squaw'. My parents expected that at private school I would be better treated by the educated persons of the community, but the element of a fair education was missing. Racism prevailed in the stereotype images of Indians that I was expected to uphold. I recall one kindly teacher prevailing on me to wear a head-band and feather she had prepared for the class picture and I remember the betrayal of friendship with some bitterness.

My family returned to the Allegany Reservation in 1939 where we lived among the Longhouse believers. My mother was treated by

37

the Medicine society and a Dark Dance was put up for her in my grandmother's house. We children were not allowed to attend, but were sent to the second floor where we tried to look down through a chimney opening in the floor. My brothers were frightened by the sounds they heard. When I read of the ceremony in *Apologies* I was amazed that Wilson had been allowed to attend with Dr. Fenton and told him that I had been uneasy reading about the ceremony in his book. Mr. Wilson asked me how I felt about reading of the Little Water ceremony and I told him that I had been unable to do so as it is a secret society of the highest order and my mother had been made a member of it. (I have since read his account of it.)

Throughout my educational experience there was nothing to reinforce Indian identity or pride of identity, so it became apparent to me that the prime purpose in educating Indians is to expedite their acculturation and assimilation. Because of the terminology used in textbooks Indians are depicted as without culture or dignity and have not encountered a favorable academic attitude toward our cultural feasibility in contemporary American life, but instead encounter the attitude that Indians are obstacles to progress. Wilson had a keen appreciation of these facts and recognized my resentment at having to make cultural sacrifices in order to get an education when afterward I did not fit properly into the value system of the dominant society.

Reading Edmund Wilson's Iroquois articles opened a door for better understanding of the Iroquois at a critical point in our history. I had long been frustrated by the ignorance of non-Indians about Indians and felt that this ignorance, combined with romantic notions about us as part of the past had been destructive by encouraging stereotyping, which is a form of racism. I was struck by Wilson's sensitivity to the nuances of language and the difficulty that he recognized, as an accomplished linguist, of translating into English the concepts of Iroquois culture. He wrote about us as the living, vibrant culture in transition that we are, he was not distracted by the common misconception among scholars that Indian cultures in transition are less valuable or valid than those encountered by the first colonists. Mr Wilson recognized that member nations of the League of the Iroquois, Mohawk – Oneida – Onondaga – Cayuga – Seneca and Tuscarora, had retained their cultural identities and value system. Wilson carefully documented the Iroquois struggle for survival in opposing projects imposed on Indian waterways and land bases against our collective wills, and which we recognized would soon liquidate our societies. Throughout *Apologies* Mr. Wilson is highly critical of the attitudes of New York State officials toward the Iroquois.

Some time after meeting Edmund Wilson I proposed that he allow me to adopt him into the Seneca Hawk clan, my hereditary clan. As a baby I had been given my Seneca name in the Longhouse by my grandmother and my children have received Seneca names in the Longhouse given by my mother and my aunt, so I consider that an adoption could have been arranged. But Edmund Wilson declined the offer. He said that unlike Fenton he had not done enough to deserve the honor and I could not convince him otherwise. I am not sure that he understood that I am opposed to the casual adoption of non-Indians at social events and that I deplore this practice. In 1965 I gave birth to a son, whom I named Antonio Edmund Wilson Mele in order to put Edmund Wilson's name on the Seneca rolls. (Every child of an enrolled Seneca woman is enrolled with the nation.) Mr. Wilson wrote that he regretted that I had given my son so many names as he had only two which were 'enough'. He also wondered if some day, when the boy grew up, he might not like his writing, but he was obviously pleased by the honor. I regret that the child is not named just Edmund Wilson Mele. To do that I felt would require Mr. Wilson's consent and I was not sure that he would give it after so modestly refusing my offer of adoption.

When Edmund Wilson visited the Allegany Reservation in 1958 it was much the same as it had been in my childhood. After the Kinzua Dam was under way Seneca home owners were offered new suburban-type dwellings in two relocation areas, eleven miles apart, to replace the simple weathered houses that Wilson had seen and visited. Today at Allegany these clusters of modern structures conceal from the casual observer any indication of Iroquian culture. Submerged under the waters of Kinzua Lake is some of the vegetation that was an inherent part of our culture and an integral part of the reservation landscape, which heretofore had been unabused.

The transition period during the construction of the dam and the relocation of the residents was disruptive of cultural life. There were reports of homes of Senecas resisting relocation being burned to the ground with all household effects while the owners were absent. For a time it appeared that the strength of tradition, which had survived for unknown generations, was diminished, but the Senecas have rallied and are now more conscious of preserving tradition and passing it on to the young. In community centers built with Kinzua reparations money, language, dance, song, arts and crafts are taught by Senecas who have not lost the old ways.

When I last saw the old stone house in Talcottville a new highway passing it had cut off a large section of the front lawn, leaving it exposed to the ugly paved expanse of four lanes. This sight saddened me and caused me to wonder if New York State authorities, with their self-righteous approach to progress, had refused to consider appeals to preserve the Wilson house as a result of his championing the Iroquois.

Edmund Wilson would be gratified to know that *Apologies to the Iroquois* is a much respected book among Indian scholars.

THE ARTIST AS CRITIC

LARZER ZIFF

❧

The Man by the Fire: Edmund Wilson and American Literature

The contrasting careers of Van Wyck Brooks (Harvard Class of 1908) and T. S. Eliot (Harvard Class of 1910) marked, Edmund Wilson observed, 'the watershed in the early nineteen hundreds in American life'. When Brooks visited England as a young man he found himself unable to shake his preoccupation with American subjects, and yielding to the concerns that haunted him he returned to his native land to become its leading cultural historian. Eliot, however, found the same England to be attractive, the motherland of the literature to which he wished to make his contribution, and he remained there and drowned his American accent. 'Eliot', wrote Wilson, 'represents the growth of an American internationalism; Brooks, as a spokesman of the twenties, the beginnings of the sometimes all too conscious American literary self-glorification which is part of our American imperialism.'

Wilson made these remarks in 1958, by which time he had clearly emerged as the American man of letters who both remained home at the heart of the nation's cultural life and yet ranged incisively over the world's great literatures. He was a devoted student of American literature but was sharply distrustful of those, principally university professors, who marketed it as equal in quality to such literatures as that of Britain. Whilst he reproved American critics for their shabby knowledge of great world literatures, however, he also took sharp issue with the social ideals toward which literary internationalism such as Eliot's tended. His sense of the high achievement of the European masters was accompanied by a suspicion of twentieth-century European societies, which, he said in

1945, still adhered to feudal molds and cramped the natural development of their members.

One hundred years earlier, Walt Whitman, also recognizing the superiority of European to American literature whilst believing in the superiority of American to European society, had proclaimed the death of the past and predicted that an entirely new literature would grow from the American condition, one that would speak to modern men and make the literature of the past archaic. Wilson believed no such thing. He adhered to the view that literary creations, grounded though they were in their authors' lives and times, were, nevertheless, timeless in their reach and scornful of national frontiers. Yet sharing Whitman's views of the relative strength of American over European society and the somewhat inverse ratio of the quality of the respective literatures, he developed a distinctive approach to his writings on American literature. One hears the same magisterial voice speaking in an essay on Henry Blake Fuller as one heard speaking on Dostoevsky. But the content of Wilson's comments on American writers is far more concerned with the very precise – almost precious – details of region, moment, and social gesture. As for Whitman so for Wilson American literature has not yet emerged from the general culture. Whitman accordingly made a chauvinistic appeal to the future; Wilson responded by examining the literature as part of the time and nation in which it was inseparably embedded.

I

In common with other notable creators, Edmund Wilson possessed a sensibility that at its intensest achieved a fusion of time and place so that a particular period took on the architectures of an edifice – had corridors, chambers, and neglected corners – and a particular locale breathed forth a history, manifested itself temporally. At the end of his career he sought to embody the fusion in his life as well as in his writing. *Patriotic Gore,* his most extended examination of the American past, was written after he had taken up residence in the Old Stone House in Talcottville, New York, a building that had been in the possession of one or another member of his family since the eighteenth century but that never before this late period in his life had been his own home. The journal of his years there, *Upstate*, reveals that the Old Stone House spoke to Wilson as do genealogical annals – spoke to him, for example, of his ancestors' break with New England two hundred years earlier – and he was assiduous in pursuing the ghosts of former occupants with which his mind, if not the house itself, was haunted. Physical location in a bypassed town, so out of the way that even his closest kin could not endure long periods of residence there, seemed a fitting accompaniment to his final labors on a book concerned not only with the American past but especially with writings from it that had, in his judgment, been neglected, and were, until he treated them, mere curiosities.

The fusion that he acted out as well as rendered in prose at the close of his career informs the great body of Wilson's writings on American themes almost from the start. The crucial term of place that entered into it was, of course, America, and the crucial term of time was the twenties.

The America of Wilson's early upbringing was a social caste, the members of which believed themselves to represent the mark of what, in a heterogeneous society, could validly be called American. It was an America of white Protestants whose ancestors had come to the continent when it was still a British colony, who had moved from the working of the land into the professions, and who had formed their taste principally on the standards of English literature. Edmund Wilson remained in this America when he attended Princeton, where those who came from outside it but who, nevertheless, attracted his growing curiosity were held only in a tentative friendship subject to instant cancellation should their difference prove too exotic.

After a brief period in journalism upon graduation, however, Wilson entered the American army and his service in the First World War resulted in a major shift in his definition of his homeland. 'My experience of the army', he recalled, 'had had on me a liberating effect. I could now get by with all kinds of people . . . many of my friends in the American army had been Irishmen, Swedes, Danes, Swiss, Belgians, and cockneys. . . . My association with all these had given me a strong contempt for the complaints about the "foreign" immigrants on the part of the old-line Americans and for the talk about the necessity for getting them "Americanized." '

This liberation had profound effects on the social ideals of the young man who returned to civilian life as a literary journalist and resident of Greenwich Village, opening his sympathy to the realities of those whose origins were far removed from British America and whose tuition had not been provided at Princeton. But America was a time as well as a place and in this dimension it remained for Wilson quite commensurate with the 'old-line' which he rejected as a social ideal. This was the America of the principal writers to his day, and he was far more concerned with its literary products than with the nascent efforts of writers from other Americas, writers such as, for example, Blacks or Jews.

In this concern, however, Wilson did not center on the classical American writers. For all his approving remarks about Hawthorne, for example, one senses he does not enjoy him, and he seems even less keen about Emerson and Thoreau. Melville and Whitman he liked to point to as fellow New Yorkers (in certain moods he enjoyed visualizing himself as but another warrior in the old American literary battle of New England vs. New York), but here again he was not disposed to extended critical discussion. Rather, his ranging mind moved from the center of the tradition to its corners, and in those corners discovered writers such as John Jay Chapman and John W. DeForest, George Washington Cable and Harold Frederic, writers who, in the main, could be related to the conditions that had formed him also. These minor writers had in common a powerful and peculiarly American moral insistence. They had attacked the inequities and hypocrisies of American life precisely because they were at the heart of it, knew all the family's secrets, and wanted better from it. One feels Wilson aligning himself with them when he writes about them, accepting identity as another old-liner whose freedom in Zion means license to be severe rather than complacent.

Such historical sympathy is what marks Wilson off most clearly from the contemporaries of the twenties with whom he otherwise shared so much. In the wake of Mencken they were engaged in an often gleeful assault on conventions with the positive aim of extending the boundaries of literary consciousness and expanding the resources of literary technique. It was, accordingly, convenient for them to accept the hypothetical enemy that Mencken had personified, the army of American 'boobs' wallowing in the mire of fundamental religion when they were not sufficiently upright to peer through the chinks in their neighbor's windowshade, ever anxious to resist the true and the beautiful because it was the different.

Wilson, however, was too close a historian to recognize this enemy although he delighted in Mencken's wielding of the cudgel against it. The dreaders of art, he realized, were to be found in one guise or another in all societies; there was nothing particularly American about the fear. In joining Mencken's view the writers of the twenties, he suspected, were opening themselves to misconceptions that could impair their work.

For one thing, their confusion of genuine moral fervor with mere priggishness robbed writers of a basic element in their tradition. Wilson became a masterful expositor of the serious-mindedness and courage that accompanied the moral zeal of such writers as, for example, Cable, writers who were in the aftermath of the twenties all too loosely dismissed as pompous and tedious. There was, Wilson showed, a greater fund of bravery behind the moral earnestness of such writers and they underwent severer social penalties than did those who were theatrically naughty or conscientiously amoral.

Another damaging consequence of the popular twenties' outlook, as Wilson exposed it, was that in imagining so convenient an enemy American writers were increasing their vulnerability to the real destroyers of art in their country. These destroyers he called 'Henry Luce and Hollywood'. In citing them he was suggesting that the writer's downfall would come more surely at the hands of those who welcomed him only to exploit him commercially than at the hands of those who resisted him. The particular serpent lurking in the bosom of the American artist was his barely suppressed desire to be recognized by the money makers and re-made into an object of mass consumption – to become an American Success. That serpent was older than Luce and Hollywood and figured, for example, as the great antagonist in Wilson's drama in *Patriotic Gore* of General Ulysses S. Grant transformed into President Ulysses S. Grant.

The crucial term of time within which Wilson found his identity and America identified itself for him was the twenties. He wrote: 'I find that I am a man of the twenties. I am still expecting something exciting: drinks, animated conversation, gaiety, brilliant writing, uninhibited exchange of ideas. I have never had quite the expectation of Scott Fitzgerald's characters that somewhere things were "glimmering"; I thought life had its excitement wherever I was. But it was part of the same *zeitgeist*.'

His membership in that generation was initially, in the very nature of the matter, accidental. He found himself at the same Princeton as Fitzgerald, Bishop, and others with literary gifts. But Wilson soon converted this into a voluntary allegiance. When he came to literary New York after his war service he worked on poetry, fiction, and drama as well as criticism and he sought the company of writers as their peer, not their chronicler. His critical voice grew stronger through repeated exercise (far from the usual fate of the weekly critic) and almost despite himself his equality with the brilliant writers of the twenties came more and more to be the achievement of his expository rather than his fictive pen. He became a shaper of the twenties as well as the shaped: the accidental friend of Fitzgerald, for example, but the deliberate searcher-out and promoter of the unknown Hemingway. Although he accepted the role of week-in and week-out schoolmaster and publicizer of his gifted contemporaries, he elevated this into a distinct, learned, and incisive office and rejected the duties of the mere annalist. The literary chronicles he refers to when he groups his reviews for republication are his own as well as those of his time. He steadfastly avoided pinning his reputation, let alone his identity, to the fortuitousness of his associations and left the job of literary gossip columnist to others who in their gossip would have also to gossip of him.

In 1943, 'retiring a little before his time' as he put it, Wilson indulged himself in the recognition that he, too, was a significant figure of the twenties, he, too, was an object for the dissertation of the graduate student and the imitation of the younger critic. Writing of himself in the third person, he said, 'The literary worker of the twenties who had recently thought of himself as merely – to change the figure – attempting to keep alive a small fire while the cold night was closing down is surprised to find himself surrounded by animals attracted or amazed by the light, some of which want to get into the warmth but others of which are afraid of him and would feel safer if they could eat him. What is strange is that he should seem to belong to a kind of professional group, now becoming extinct and a legend, in which the practice of letters was a common motivation.'

The words are spoken with a certain arrogance, to be sure, exacerbated, one suspects, by a thousand petty petitions, but they are grounded in a characteristic sureness of mind. The man of letters is the product of his times and his direct presence is not available to those who did not undergo the same shaping. The profoundest influence the twenties had, then, on Wilson as a critic of American writing was to fix in his mind the inescapable inter-dependence of a man and his generation, a reflexive relationship of equal power with that between a man and his physical surroundings. He rejected the notion of the isolated artist and looked always for his times and his associates in him. Van Wyck Brooks's studies of American literary history interested him because they provided writers with such contexts, and he himself early developed a sense that his good fortune in being a part of the twenties may have been different in degree but was not different in kind from the sense of generation that sustained earlier American writers. During Wilson's youth the story of American literature was frequently represented as the tale of isolate souls, a saga of giants crippled and marooned in a sea of hostility: Melville self-exiled in New York as effectively as if he had gone to the Galapagos, for example; or Whitman insulated by a mindless coterie in shabby Camden. His experience in the twenties told Wilson that this could not be so even before his researches showed him that it was not so. He knew what

49

food the artist must have had if he had grown to the strength he exhibited.

Closely connected with this belief was his perception that the American writer had never been either so exclusively non-European as Brooks would have it or so recently American as Percy Lubbock would have it. Lewis, Dos Passos, Faulkner, and Hemingway, Wilson maintained, 'have obviously owed as much to European writers and European travel as Hawthorne and Howells had done and, if the stories of Sherwood Anderson grew up, like his native grass, without any foreign fertilizer, so had those of Mark Twain, who belonged to the Howells era.'

Wilson converted these convictions into a splendid lesson in *The Shock of Recognition* which appeared in 1943, the year in which he pictured himself dramatically as a survivor of the warm twenties in a time of general frost. That remarkable anthology buried once and for all the persisting view that the American literary past was a series of flashes – some brilliant, most but a spark – emitted by men of talent against a wall of darkness. Wilson's 'chronicle of the progress of literature in the United States' took its title from Melville's assertion, prompted by his reading of Hawthorne's stories, that 'Genius, all over the world, stands hand in hand, and one shock of recognition runs the whole circle round.' Always mindful of the universality insisted upon by Melville, Wilson nevertheless centered his anthology (1290 pages full, so that, alas, it has been allowed to go out of print) on documents that revealed the awareness the American had of his fellow writers and of his region.

'What I am trying to present, in fact,' Wilson wrote in the Fore-word, 'is the developing self-consciousness of the American genius from the moment in the middle of the last century when we first really had a literature worth talking about.' His execution went somewhat beyond the intent to reveal that American writing acquired a cultural density both from the larger connections of genius speaking to genius and the smaller but nevertheless intensive liaisons and enmities formed on the battlefield of literary politics. In such a scheme poetasters as well as poets were allowed to speak.

In *The Shock of Recognition* documents are introduced and ordered in such a way that the whole which emerges is larger than the sum of its parts, which is to say that although it is an anthology it is the very best in its genre and therefore ultimately leaps out of its genre. The selections cohere into an original, imaginative, single work. Wilson's headnotes are masterpieces of that constantly abused sub-species of literary scholarship, and the length that limits the book's current availability is the result of a firm insistence upon reproducing the whole of every selected piece.

Patriotic Gore arrived almost twenty years later as the second and last of Wilson's book-length works devoted to American writings, and it is, of course, a critical history rather than an anthology. Still, the resemblance between the two is strong with *Patriotic Gore* tending toward anthology even as *The Shock of Recognition* tends toward history. As has been noted, when Wilson centered exclusively on American authors he departed from the perspective he brought to other literatures in a concentration on the culture that was continuous with the literature, and one strong mark of this is his care to provide long quotations not so much in lieu of critical interpretation nor in documentary support of it as in evocation of the faded accent. He shapes social context and analyses personality finally to form an opening into which he introduces the voice of the subject concerned as the ultimate tone of the values under discussion. *Patriotic Gore* is akin to an anthology, one in which the incisive headnotes and long selections of *The Shock of Recognition* are replaced by long, involved headnotes and brief but eloquent quotations.

'It may, however, be worthwhile to do justice to its author,' writes Wilson of DeForest, 'by rescuing from *Justine* and *The Wetherel Affair* – both hard to get hold of nowadays and unlikely to be read in the future by anyone except literary historians – a few memorable character sketches.' More than ten pages of quotation follow.

For all of Wilson's alert modernity, *Patriotic Gore* has, thus, a curiously old-fashioned flavor reminiscent of that of the nineteenth-century bibliophile who wrote about ignored books that intrigued him from the assumption that his task was not so much to call the attention of scholars to them as to attach them once again to the consciousness of a reading public. In providing this flavor Wilson is implicitly correcting the widening battalions of professors of American literature who in unearthing minor authors and exposing them in monographs written in a quasi-scientific academic code are, in effect, moving those authors from a simple earthen tomb to a hideous plastic crypt. Wilson's voice is for the ears of the general reader, in whose existence he believed because his career had been devoted to creating him, and it says to him, here in my pages that which flowered so briefly may still be recaptured, but, despite my efforts, the fading is inevitable; my final justification is that it has accounted to me for some part of myself and may so serve you.

Only American writing seems to have tempted Wilson to so personal an approach, to have brought him so close to the authorial glance from the library window or the undramatic melancholy of a cleric of the past century contemplating the paling rhetoric of a once consequential synod of yet an earlier century. He unhesitatingly used the pronoun 'our' when talking of that writing; he was an American addressing Americans about a wider reality they could share if they would but take care. Although *The Shock of Recognition* and *Patriotic Gore* have informed readers beyond America, and, it can confidently be assumed, will continue to do so, unlike Edmund Wilson's work in other areas these books have a further meaning for Americans. They are the literary equivalent of a message to the faithful which the ecclesiastical outsider understands and may even admire but which assumes for its fullest effect a common cultural experience as much as an intelligent mind.

II

At the outset of the twenties, aware of the promise of his remarkable generation but yet to experience its fruition, Wilson wrote a poem he called 'A Perverse Thought'. In it he evoked what he imagined to be the atmosphere of fin-de-siècle literary New York, an atmosphere which he, as a young journalist in a far more dynamic New York was, nevertheless, encountering at unexpected turns of corner or in secluded armchairs. His fascination with this older New York made tolerable for him the scarcely tolerable behavior of his supervising editor on *Vanity Fair*, Frank Crowninshield, since Crowninshield, for all his shortcomings, Wilson saw, was a guide to the era of Richard Watson Gilder and William Dean Howells whose ghosts still flickered in the shadows of the editorial room. With this fascination he was more interested to improve an opportunity to lunch with the forgotten John Jay Chapman at his club than to sit at the Algonquin amidst the coruscations of Robert Benchley and Dorothy Parker.

The poem, dated 29 August 1920, began:

> Sometimes I wish I had been born
> Among that calm race of 'ladies and gentlemen'
> Who thought Bayard Taylor a great poet
> And took chaste joy in visiting Rome.

The reader of Wilson's childhood memories, *A Prelude*, can recognize beyond the 'perversity' of this wish to inhabit a more decorous and self-assured age even at the expense of its having been distinctly mediocre, the fact that the poet actually was, in good part, the involuntary heir of that age's values even before he consciously sought out its survivors. Before the great war Wilson had gone abroad with mother, aunt, and cousin in their pleated, long-waisted blouses and large flowered hats, and with father and uncle in white waistcoats and spats. They had toured a Europe in which spas figured more prominently than museums and in which the joys they sought were located at a distance from those of the barracks and bordello which enlivened the first experience of Europe for most members of Wilson's generation.

To a large extent, then, Wilson was of the 'calm race,' but as the poet of 'A Perverse Thought' he says that his life 'has been one long anger/Against the meanness and ugliness of my times'. This is self-dramatizing at the least if one recalls that the writer was but twenty-five and had at home, at Princeton, and even in the army (where his politically influential father had, at one point, arranged a change to a more comfortable posting for him) a relatively unmean and unugly existence.

But if the lines are inaccurate as summary they are valuable as prediction of the career that was to follow in the next two decades. Like other writers before him, and most specifically like the Stephen Crane who had really inhabited fin-de-siècle New York, Wilson's fictional autobiography revealed far more about the road he longed to take than the one he had already traveled, and did so by reversing the two and representing the accomplished as the longed-for and the sought as the achieved.

Six years later with the twenties already showing its capacity to become the stuff of legends. Wilson attempted a temporary assessment of its literary achievement, a sort of up-to-the-moment line score of a game still in progress. His effort is remarkable for the soundness of judgement displayed. Wilson the weekly critic had so developed his historical consciousness that he could step from the melee and view its principal participants with detached wisdom. The fifty years that have passed since have done far more to validate than revise his opinions and to underline his remarkable capacity both to live in the moment and to see it as history. In addition to giving marks to his contemporaries, Wilson in his essay, 'The All-Star Literary Vaudeville', viewed them collectively and, with an awareness of cultural continuity that seemed his exclusive possession (although his contemporaries may very well be excused on the ground that they had prudently come to rely upon Wilson as their historical conscience), he warned them that whatever boundaries of the last generation they had passed they had not necessarily surpassed that generation.

'When we consider Henry James, Stephen Crane, and even such novelists of the second rank as George W. Cable and William Dean Howells,' he pointed out, ' . . . we are struck with certain superiorities over our race of writers today. It may be said of these men in general, that, though their ideas were less "emancipated", they possessed a sounder culture than we; and, though less lively, they were better craftsmen. They were professional men of letters, and they had thoroughly learned their trade.' He called special attention to Stephen Crane 'whose work astonishes us now by an excellence of quality by no means incomparable – as how much of our present fiction is? – to the best European work in the same kind.'

If the two may be separated theoretically at least, Wilson the practical critic addressed himself to standards of craftsmanship whilst Wilson the historical conscience addressed himself to those aspects of the inheritance that were needed by the American culture of his day if it was to realize its best self. He had more of the calm race in him than he cared to make explicit and his enjoyment of his ride on the carousel of the twenties though it shook him free of moralistic pieties never freed him from a profound respect for moral earnestness. Even when he is in the thick of the fray at a Village party or in simultaneous debate with the Communists and the Conservatives, even when he is literally unbuttoned, Wilson conveys still an impression of collar and tie, a feeling that truth to self must deep down be truth to origins.

III

The American literary genius who spoke most tellingly out of the past to Wilson and who served for him as the symbol of devotion to craftsmanship and concern for the maintenance of a rigorous standard of literary culture was Edgar Allan Poe. He, if any single writer, was Edmund Wilson's daemon.

For all the wraithlike quality Poe had, even for his contemporaries, his first and perhaps most important lesson for Wilson was solidly practical. Wilson could look back over a modest list of first-rate American writers but Poe alone among them sought to sustain himself through journalism as Wilson sought to sustain himself. 'My principal heroes among journalists in English have been De Quincey, Poe and Shaw, and they have all, in their various manners, shown themselves masters of these arts,' he wrote. 'Poe in particular – though at the cost of an effort which was one of the pressures that shattered him – succeeded in selling almost all he wrote to the insipid periodicals of his day.'

What the scholarly and the gentlemanly took to be Poe's duplicity in marketing the same or a slightly altered piece as separate works, or in reprinting successive versions of a composition as separate compositions, Wilson saw as not just a valid professional procedure if the writer would wrest a living from his sensibility

C

but as a strategy to be followed. It is to Poe, therefore, more than to any other single example that we may attribute the unapologetic recurrence of certain of Wilson's essays, initially paid journalistic reviews, in different collections of essays under different titles. The world may not owe the man of letters a living, but the man of letters owes one to himself.

Less practically Poe symbolized for Wilson the capacity of the American writer to become a figure of western culture rather than an entry in the national history. 'His works,' Wilson felt, 'bear no conceivable relation, either external or internal, to the life of the people.' Rather it was Poe who was the great consolidator of the perception that 'it is not what you say that counts, but what you make the reader feel (he always italicizes the word "effect"); no one understood better than Poe that the deepest psychological truth may be rendered through phantasmagoria. Even the realistic stories of Poe are, in fact, only phantasmagoria of a more circumstantial kind.'

On this level, of course, Poe did not serve as a figure from the American past but as a landless harbinger of the modern temper, and as such he received the most crucial attention from Wilson in *Axel's Castle*. The avidity with which the French literary intelligence absorbed Poe could only have been encouragement to a relatively unknown American critic contemplating a book on symbolism that would lead him into a foreign literature so jealously tended by its inheritors as was that of France.

Wilson's strategy of quotation also owes something to Poe's critical habits. Obviously Poe as an underpaid reviewer was hard pressed to produce more words each week than was comfortable for him and fell back on quotation as a respite just as other reviewers, Wilson among them, would do. But to rest here is to trivialize. Anyone who grasps Poe's theory of effect recognizes that its great apparent shortcoming is that it does not seem to apply to most of the major literature to Poe's time. One of Poe's central tasks, therefore, was to show that the conventional literary classics actually achieved their strength despite rather than because of their length. He dissected long poems or full novels in search of their emotional components and the demonstration of his thesis resided ultimately in his providing the quotations that would uncover specific effects. Quotation became revelation in Poe's best criticism as it was to become in Wilson's.

Nowhere can one find Poe the model reviewer more strikingly set forth than in *The Shock of Recognition*, a great pupil's tribute to his master. To read the Poe review of Margaret Fuller in the context Wilson supplies is indeed to experience at least the minor shock of recognizing what Poe meant by the superiority of a subjectiveness that 'paints a scene less by its features than its effects.' The quotation Poe supplies leaps into relief and the reader realizes the way in which words affect him. In *The Shock of Recognition* Poe's quotation from Fuller is a quotation within a quotation since Wilson, as it were, is quoting Poe, and the reflexive images that are sent vibrating link minor contemporary with major contemporary, the past with the present, the subjective with the modern, and American provincial with the world.

But finally as one contemplates Edmund Wilson's writings on American literature one is forced back to the observation that his interest extended itself at greatest length when it encountered the minor and neglected rather than the major; that, without losing his strongly modern sense of presence or forgetting the range of literatures he had traversed, Wilson did, nevertheless, in *Patriotic Gore*, yield to the attractions of the regional and the antiquarian; that, whereas in dealing with other literatures he is concerned with the transparency of national boundaries, dealing with American literature Wilson becomes hypnotized by the pertinacity of local boundaries – not just those which mark off the New Englander from the New Yorker nor even those that separate the upstate New Yorker from the city New Yorker, but precisely those that make of the Albany New Yorker yet another category. Poe, and after him Crane, both of whom were tied to New York periodical publishing, served as great exemplars of craftsmanship but in their bizarre daily doings they were to be admired rather than imitated. Psychologically they may have been the doppelgangers of the Wilson whose private life is now emerging in the posthumous journals, but the public critic had a powerful sense of his membership in a more cautious American tradition and a powerful desire to recover that part of the American past down to its nicest particular that would meet his sense of his tradition.

Beyond this, however, the appeal on Edmund Wilson of such writers as Harold Frederic and Henry Blake Fuller, on whom, finally, he expended more writing than on major figures including Poe leads to speculation. Did the great master of American critics ruefully forbode that time would relegate him to the rank of Cable, DeForest, and Chapman? *Patriotic Gore* has at times, and especially read now after Wilson's death, the effect of Louis MacNeice's 'Elegy for Minor Poets', the first lines of which say:

> Who often found their way to pleasant meadows
> Or maybe once to a peak, who saw the Promised Land,
> Who took the correct three strides but tripped their hurdles,

and which concludes,

> In spite of and because of which, we later
> Suitors to their mistress (who, unlike them, stays young)
> Do right to hang on the grave of each a trophy
> Such as, if solvent, he would himself have hung
> Above himself; these debtors preclude our scorn –
> Did we not underwrite them when we were born?

MacNeice now is regarded as a minor poet, an attractive also-ran in heats won by Eliot and Auden, and therefore a poet who was prudent when he provided his own elegy. Was some such instinct moving beneath the thoughtful prose of *Patriotic Gore*?

It is difficult not to feel it there in the successive pictures of Americans who lived so intensely, meant so much to their contemporaries, and yet left so little that compels now by its mere presence. Leon Edel reminds us of Wilson's impatience, tempered with sadness, at being praised as an expositor at the expense of his novels. The elegiac note in his writings on Americans whose names have faded may have been struck from him by this: that he as well as Fitzgerald was a novelist of the twenties; that he as well as Lawrence pushed back the fences that cramped the representation of sexual love in literature. His undoubted sovereignty as a critic and historian may not have sufficed to balance the neglect of his fictions, and in his criticism, therefore, he developed a corresponding sensitivity to the neglected.

Perhaps Wilson in his image of himself as the man by the fire was unfair to the animals that crouched outside the circle of light and so unfair to himself. He may have underestimated their desire to perpetuate him. We thank him for the minor men he has restored to us but we lack reason to number him among them.

PETER SHARRATT

❧

Edmund Wilson and France

Michel de Montaigne once wrote that he would willingly come back from beyond the grave to contradict anyone who described him other than he really was in life. As I begin to write about Edmund Wilson and France I am reminded of his remarks in *I Thought of Daisy* about the danger of using a writer's random notes and occasional writings after his death and 'constructing a system which would have filled the writer with horror'. For someone who did not know Wilson personally but has made his acquaintance only from his books the danger is all the greater. Yet when memories have faded (or become erroneously exact) it is the written word which will remain. I shall moreover base most of what I have to say on two of his major studies, and a number of solid essays, and do my best not to make too much of the asides; and, when I have looked at what he says on the subject of French thought and literature, I shall try to draw a biographical grid on which to superimpose his readings in French, and see if some consistent picture emerges.

Edmund Wilson's two best-known books are, I suppose, *Axel's Castle* and *To the Finland Station*. Now, since about half of the one and a quarter of the other talk about French literature and ideas, and since, over the years of his long career as a journalist, this interest appeared in numerous articles and reviews, and was never entirely abandoned, it is worth considering the extent of his involvement with France and French culture.

The two books I have mentioned grew directly and consciously out of his journalistic activities in the twenties. In 'Thoughts on Being Bibliographed' (1944, in *Classics and Commercials*, 1950) he acknowledged an overall debt to James Huneker, an American journalist of an earlier generation who had communicated to Americans a knowledge and appreciation of European literature and music of the preceding fifty years. Because of Huneker much could now be taken for granted.

> There remained for the young journalist, however, two roads that had still to be broken: the road to the understanding of the most recent literary events in the larger international world – Joyce, Eliot, Proust, etc. – which were already out of the range of readers the limits of whose taste had been fixed by *Egoists* and *The Quintessence of Ibsenism*; and to bring home to the 'bourgeois' intellectual world the most recent developments of Marxism in connection with the Russian Revolution. I was of course far from being either alone or first in popularizing either of these subjects; but they were the matters with which I was mostly concerned, and I felt that what I was doing had some logical connection with the work of the older men I admired.

It is good to have Wilson's own explanation of the origin and similarity of purpose of the two books and to read his modest disclaimers.

Axel's Castle ('A Study in the Imaginative Literature of 1870–1930') takes up, whether consciously or not, where Henry James's *History of French Literature* left off, and is indeed a work of synthesis and of 'communication'. It aims to make French symbolism known to a much wider public, to define its existence as a literary movement, and to establish links between writers of French and English (Yeats, Valéry, Eliot, Proust, Joyce and Stein) which had not been perceived so clearly before. Clarity and simplicity run through the book, combined with vividness in the presentation of men and ideas. This is particularly welcome in the treatment of Mallarmé and Valéry. The delicate yet persistent flavour of Wilson's criticism may be sampled in the passage in which he compares Mallarmé and his disciple:

> Yet Paul Valéry, when we put him beside Mallarmé, whom

61

he echoes in these poems so often, is seen to possess the more vigorous intellect and the more solid imagination. Mallarmé is always a painter, usually a watercolourist – he wrote verses for ladies' fans as he might have painted little figures and flowers on them. He has his brightness and relief, but it is only such brightness and relief as is possible to someone working in the flat – whereas Valéry's genius is sculptural rather: these mythological poems have a density of cloud-shapes heavily massed – if they were not clouds, we should call them marmoreal. He gives us figures and groups half disengaged – and he runs to effects less of colour than of light: the silvery, the sombre, the sunny, the translucent, the crystalline. And his verses carry off with the emphasis of an heroic resounding diction reminiscent of Alfred de Vigny the fluid waverings, the coy ambiguities and the delicately caught nuances which he has learned from Mallarmé.

These rather precious comparisons are aptly illustrated by the poems which Wilson quotes, containing, he says, 'some of the most original poetry ever written'. It soon becomes clear, however, that there is much in Valéry he finds unsatisfactory, *La Jeune Parque* for example, because of its confusion, and because it is not quite reducible either to a description of incidents or to mere thoughts. Valéry's prose he likes even less, finding it incomprehensible and devoid of ideas. 'We find simply,' he writes, 'as we do in his poetry, the presentation of intellectual situations, instead of the development of lines of thought', as a result of the author's dabbling in the new scientific and mathematical theories, and using them snobbishly to cover up his own deficiencies. Wilson was irritated above all by Valéry's address to the French Academy when he succeeded to Anatole France's chair, a straightforward attack on his predecessor instead of the customary eulogy. He dwells on this discourtesy, partly because his admiration for Valéry's intelligence and origin-ality fell far short of idolatry, and partly because France was one of his favourite authors, a fellow-journalist who 'represented that French tradition of classical lucidity and simplicity against which the Symbolists were rebelling'. When Wilson writes 'Anatole

France was a popular writer: he aimed to be persuasive and intelligible . . . [he] was essentially a rationalist: he did not deny the
incongruities and incoherences of experience, but he attempted to
write about them, at least, in a simple, logical and harmonious style',
his identification with him is almost complete. The chapter closes
with a comparison between Valéry's M. Teste (who, like Leonardo
da Vinci, was for Valéry 'a symbol of the pure intellect, of
the human consciousness turned in upon itself') and France's
M. Bergeret of the *Histoire contemporaine*, 'a social being, polite,
agreeable and fond of company'. M. Bergeret, in the later volumes,
like Wilson and unlike Valéry, is warmly and actively interested in
the community and its civilization.

After Eliot (the French influence on whom is discussed at length)
we come to Proust, who is included because he was 'the first
important novelist to apply the principles of Symbolism in fiction'.
Once more it gradually becomes clear that Wilson does not find
his author entirely sympathetic, and eventually loses patience with
him for his 'peculiar kind of overcultivated and fundamentally
unconvincing sensibility', and for his decadence.

> Proust is perhaps the last great historian of the loves, the
> society, the intelligence, the diplomacy, the literature and
> the art of the Heartbreak House of capitalist culture; and the
> little man with the sad appealing voice, the metaphysician's
> mind, the Saracen's beak, the ill-fitting dress-shirt and the
> great eyes that seem to see all about him like the many-faceted
> eyes of a fly, dominates the scene and plays host in the mansion
> where he is not long to be master.

As with Valéry and Proust, Wilson's enthusiasm for James Joyce
and Gertrude Stein (both symbolists who lived in Paris) with their
brilliant and original conceptions, is dampened by his exasperation
at their tediousness and pedantic mystification. With all these
writers, at the same time as he expounds their originality, he points
to the elements of decay and decline which are already present. He
briefly alludes to the development of Symbolism into Dadaism and
eventually into Surrealism; here it is no longer their poetry which

interests him, but their social–revolutionary attitudes and their political journalism.

The book has been working its way towards a contrast between Arthur Rimbaud and the Axel of Villiers de l'Isle-Adam's work of this name (1890). Wilson retells the story of the beautiful and virile Count Axel of Auersburg with his incredibly vast hidden treasure, of his love for Sara and their joint rapturous suicide. Axel, in his complete isolation from the world, and withdrawal into the inner world of symbols and fleshless delights, is seen as a typical symbolist hero, very different from Rimbaud, the exotic adventurer, and visionary author of *Une Saison en enfer*, who made several unsuccessful attempts to escape from Europe to the East.

> The other poets of whom I have been writing were as little at home in their nineteenth-century world as Rimbaud, and they were mostly as disillusioned with its enthusiasms; but they had remained in it and managed to hold their places in it by excreting, like patient molluscs, iridescent shells of literature – whereas Rimbaud, with genius equal to any's, with genius perhaps superior to any's, had rejected Europe altogether – not merely its society and ideas, but even the kind of sensibility which one cultivated when one tried to live at odds with it and the kind of literature this sensibility supplied – getting away to a life of pure action and a more primitive civilization.

The conclusion of *Axel's Castle* is that neither Axel's nor Rimbaud's brands of escapism are worth cultivating (though it should be said that Wilson himself has more than a little of each). 'Axel's world of the private imagination in isolation from the life of society', he writes 'seems to have been exploited and explored as far as for the present is possible' (the French New Novelists of the fifties were to prove that it *was* possible to exploit and explore it much further), and Rimbaud's solution does not work because we cannot obliterate our machine-ridden and standardized world. Wilson seems to be feeling his way towards accepting that literature will now (this is the end of the twenties) have a social–realist cast.

In the meantime, western Europe has been recovering from

64

the exhaustion and despair of the War; and in America the comfortable enjoyment of what was supposed to be American prosperity, which since the War has made it possible for Americans to accept with a certain complacency the despondency as well as the resignation of European books, has given way to a sudden disquiet. And Americans and Europeans are both becoming more and more conscious of Russia, a country where a central social–political idealism has been able to use and to inspire the artist as well as the engineer.

Axel's Castle is still widely read, almost fifty years after it was first published. Wilson's insights, his obvious enjoyment of the books he is writing about, even his exasperation at their shortcomings, his ability to perceive what links such different writers together, his personal blend of anecdote, character-sketch, physical description and broad generalization, all combine to ensure that he will appeal to new readers. It is one of those classics of criticism which can be read either as an introduction, or to refresh one's mind or memory; it is in no sense a history of this literary movement, nor does it contain a ponderous argument with a full supporting cast of professors and doctors. And it is exquisitely written.

After the publication of *Axel's Castle*, throughout the thirties and especially after 1934, Wilson turned not so much to politically motivated literature, though he was interested in this, as to political and social thought and the history of the idea of revolution. In 1935 he was able to make a trip to Russia and to spend five months there. In 1940 he published the fruits of these years of research and reflection in *To the Finland Station*, which is, as the subtitle states, 'A Study in the Writing and Acting of History'. The starting-point is the discovery by Michelet in 1824 of Vico's *Scienza Nuova* published in 1725. Talking of this work of Vico's in *The Intent of the Critic* in 1941, Wilson says that it was 'a revolutionary work on the philosophy of history, in which he asserted for the first time that the *social world* was *certainly the work of man*, and attempted what is, so far as I know, the first social interpretation of a work of literature'. But in *To the Finland Station* it is Michelet, not Vico, with whom he is concerned. What he admires in his historical writing is his realism and rationalism; he is less enthusiastic about his romanticism and his rhetoric. The mature Michelet, he notes, like Balzac 'had the novelist's social interest and grasp of character, the poet's imagination and passion', an apt enough description of Wilson's own writing here as in *Axel's Castle*. The titles of the chapters ('Michelet Discovers Vico' or 'Karl Marx Dies at His Desk' for example) smack of early novels, or newspaper headlines; Wilson's essays, like his novels, owe much to his journalism. In *The History of France*, which he praises perhaps excessively, the chief character in the story is the people, 'humanity creating itself'. Michelet, too, had had to create himself since he did not belong to any professional caste, and had made his own way. Wilson is less sympathetic to Taine and Renan because although they were at first rejected by their colleagues they eventually became accepted as sages in their society. He sees in them already a decline in the writing of history. Renan is given high praise for his *Origins of Christianity* ('perhaps the greatest of all histories of ideas') but Wilson considers his prose disappointingly pale, mechanical and soporific, with definite signs of decadence. Yet he is not at ease with him, and indeed it is not clear what Renan is doing here. Even Taine, whom he finds more congenial, is included not so much as a social historian, as because his *History of English Literature* had profoundly influenced Wilson. In *The Intent of the Critic* he tells us that he had read it when he was at school and that it was responsible for his own critical outlook, providing him with his historical approach to literary criticism. In any case Taine turns out to be a professional snob who is scathing of his predecessors and writes in a mechanistic style. Last in this odd line of nineteenth-century historians is Anatole France, author of the fictitious *Histoire contemporaine*, and other historical novels or romanced histories. It is not surprising that Wilson finds these unsatisfactory as history, because of a lack of direction and purpose. In his 1971 Introduction to a new edition of the book Wilson admits that he has not done justice to Anatole France here, and that on re-reading the *Histoire contemporaine* he finds it 'still a surprisingly accurate picture of French politics and society in our own day'. With France he ends his brief account of the historians of the bourgeois revolution; after this, he explains, the tradition, whose lurching progress he has followed from Vico to France, disintegrates completely.

At this stage in the book there is a chronological break and a return to the end of the eighteenth century and a study of the early history of French socialism. Wilson seems to enjoy this more than talking about the bourgeois historians, of whom, with the exception of Michelet, he does not entirely approve. When he comes to write about the early socialists he continues, as a practising writer, to be struck with the different kinds of rhetoric they use. He starts with Gracchus Babeuf, 'the last of the real French revolutionaries', and the speech he made in his own defence, just before his execution in 1797. The speech, says Wilson, 'has a realism and sobriety which suggest much later phases of socialism. It is no longer the rhetoric of the Revolution, grandiose, passionate and confusing. . . . It has moments of grandeur which it is not absurd to compare to Socrates' *Apology*.' After Babeuf we digress a little to look at the Comte de Saint-Simon, visionary, impossible idealist perhaps even lunatic, before we come to Fourier and Owen and their literary counterpart Shelley. Once more Wilson shows how alive he was to the way they wrote:

> All were distinguished by lives of a pure and philosophical eccentricity; by a rarefied rhetoric which today seems inspired; and by fundamental social insights which were to remain of the highest value. We have seen in such later French historians as Michelet, Renan and Taine, how this rhetoric was to grow more gaudy and to solidify in hypostasized abstractions.

I wish Wilson had said more about Fourier (though the relevance of this in a history of socialism is debatable) but I suspect that he did not find him attractive. Fourier's honesty, lucidity and piety he admired, but not the messianic madness nor the iconoclasm which were later to appeal to André Breton, as can be seen in his *Ode à Charles Fourier* of 1947. Just as Wilson, for all his enlightened and libertarian principles, scorned the nihilistic and anti-social character of Dadaism, and the anarchy of Surrealism, so he could not accept Fourier's impassioned rejection of the old constraints, nor the new ones he imposed to ensure the birth of Harmony. Yet I am sure that he would have loved *Le Nouveau Monde amoureux*, which was not published until 1967.

The conclusion to this section of the book contains an account of the establishment and spread of the Fourierist communities in America, and of Etienne Cabet's *Voyage en Icarie*. One reason for the success of these utopias was the feeling that even a revolution could not have saved Europe from decline, and that salvation lay in America.

We have already seen something similar at the end of *Axel's Castle*. The decline of Europe was a thought often in Wilson's mind and we shall return to it.

With this we must leave the French historians and socialists. It may seem that Wilson has covered the ground rather hastily, and it is true, as reviewers were quick to tell him, that his account of French socialists of the second half of the century is threadbare to say the least; but it is rather that these Frenchmen represent the first stations on the long journey to St. Petersburg, too familiar to excite his attention for long as he speeds on to his destination. But he has shown the parallel development of an idea in theory and practice and, although the destination is Russia, the subject is the origin of communism. This explains the lengthy exposition of the thought of Marx and Engels – a part of the journey where the train appears to slow down, and we have leisure to familiarize ourselves with the new and unexplored countryside. It is the Rhineland which provides the link with the French social ideas, since it was there that Marx was a contributor to, and eventually an editor of, the *Rheinische Zeitung*. Both Marx and Engels gradually lose their germanness, and become classless and international. Yet they are close observers of the continuing French revolution. Wilson stresses the importance of *The Class Struggles in France (1848–50)*, which Marx wrote in London and published in the *Revue der Neuen Rheinischen Zeitung*, and above all *The Eighteenth Brumaire of Louis Bonaparte* (1852), and *The Civil War in France* (1871), which analyses the Commune. 'These writings of Marx are electrical', he comments. 'Nowhere perhaps in the history of thought is the reader so made to feel the excitement of a new intellectual discovery.' The Paris Commune of 1871 is rightly seen as 'a pivotal event in European political thought'. After it there will be two distinct ways of looking at history, the bourgeois and the socialist. Wilson remarks that it is significant that people who know all about Robespierre's reign of terror are unaware that in 1871 the government were worse.

With this I must step off the train, long before it reaches the Finland station. Marx and Engels belong to a no man's land. They are in truth citizens of the world, rather than of Germany or of their countries of exile or even of Europe. I must leave them and return to France.

Wilson's interest in French literature was not confined to the two major books we have been considering. There are several other French authors who captured his attention, in particular, Malraux, Sade, Flaubert and Sartre, and whom he discussed in articles and reviews, especially in the *New Republic* and the *New Yorker*. Most of these have been republished in hardback form in the various collections, and, as Wilson himself wished, I shall refer to these revised versions, while giving the date of the original article. The French writer who intrigued him the most was undoubtedly André Malraux. He commented on his work as early as August 1933, in the *New Republic* (*Shores of Light*, 1952) at a time when nobody in America had yet discovered him, when he had published little apart from *La Condition humaine* and *Les Conquérants*, and before the latter had been translated into English. He stresses that Malraux stands aside from the classical French tradition, and from the suffocating literary coteries of Paris. You even, he says, forget that the author is French. Malraux wrote to him, acknowledging his comments, and adding that he followed with interest the fortunes of the *New Republic*. In 1935 they met in Paris when Wilson was on his way back from Russia. In *The Triple Thinkers* he talks about Malraux's alternating between long-range revolutionary fiction, and political action in Spain. Malraux seems to fill the gap, we might think, which is described at the end of *Axel's Castle*; even if his adventuring is escapist, it has a clear social and political aim. After the second war, in *Europe Without Baedeker*, he makes a comparison between Malraux and Ignazio Silone, talking especially about *La*

Lutte avec l'Ange. Although he feels that this novel is rather spoiled by overwriting and congestion, he praises it for its 'passages of sinewy and searching thought, [and] strokes of dramatic imagination'. Malraux and Silone stand alone as first-rate writers in Europe who have kept in touch with the social developments lying behind national conflicts. In an article in the *New Yorker* about the same time (1947, *Classics and Commercials*, 1950), 'George Grosz in the United States', he mentions Malraux in connection with a retrospective album of Grosz's. The similarity, not evident at first sight, is the despair and anguish which they both portray, coupled with the dominating and reassuring craftsmanship of the artist. In another article four years later, 'André Malraux: The Museum without Walls' (1951, *The Bit Between My Teeth*, 1965) he writes that the art criticism of his *Psychologie de l'art* 'is not simply one of his best productions but perhaps one of the really great books of our time', in spite of some defects in style and exposition, because of its range, grasp and allusiveness, and the enquiry it sets up into the purpose of mankind. Wilson places it in the class of Gibbon's *Decline and Fall*, *Das Kapital* and *War and Peace*. By bringing together startling photographs of art from all places and periods Malraux has been able to say something about man's attempt to control the world, and has helped to explain the contemporary intellectual and moral chaos. In *The Bit Between My Teeth* Wilson brings the essay up to date by discussing a new one-volume edition of the work called *Les Voix du Silence* which appeared after his own article in 1951. This essay is one of the best Wilson wrote. He sympathizes with Malraux's original, non–academic and passionate involvement with men and ideas, and with his versatility and his readiness to show the links between apparently disparate fields of research. Above all he admires Malraux's new and forward-looking humanism.

In later years Wilson became interested in the work of the Marquis de Sade, and many of the articles he wrote during the fifties give evidence of this. One long article 'The Vogue of the Marquis de Sade' (1952, *The Bit Between My Teeth*, 1965) contains a substantial critical exposition of his work, tracing the contemporary interest in him back to the selections published by Apollinaire, to the Dadaists who 'delighted in him as a blaster of inhibitions, and broke down the inhibition against mentioning his name', and to the Surrealists. Wilson is fascinated by Sade's attitude to the revolution, his imprisonment and his escape from execution because of the fall of Robespierre, and his pamphleteering. His work *La Philosophie dans le boudoir*, for example, contains a long pamphlet entitled 'Français! Encore un effort si vous voulez être républicains' in which we can see the link between 'Sade's own rebellious materialism and the idealism of the Revolution'. Wilson reprimands the author of one of the books he is reviewing for trying to white-wash Sade and turn him into a charming gentleman: 'So let us not try to disguise the congenital, the compulsive and inveterate sadism of the life and works of the Marquis de Sade'. His merit in Wilson's eyes is his scientific concern for his own and related problems which guarantee him an important place in the history of western thought: the second war had brought home to many (such as Camus in *L'Homme révolté*) that Sade's distorted imaginings were less vivid than real life. Wilson calls to mind the sadistic idealists of the Terror, Hitler, whom he likens to Sade's insane chemist on Etna in *La Nouvelle Justine*, and the Marxists of his own day. One of his preoccupations, both in *To the Finland Station* and in various articles, was the sullying and destruction of the Marxist ideal by the practice of cruelty and suppression. In a further article (undated, *The Bit Between My Teeth*, 1965), 'The Documents on the Marquis de Sade', he modifies his position after further readings in Sade, finding him less acceptable and less agreeable; his trouble, he thinks, was 'psychological impotence'. While disagreeing roundly with those of Sade's commentators who talk about his literary master-pieces, he finds in Sade much to satisfy him, above all the classless, idyllic, natural utopia (here we rejoin the early socialists) of *Aline et Valcour, ou le Roman philosophique*, which is a repudiation of the vileness of European civilization. All in all, we have here a lucid and not unkind assessment of Sade's life, his character, his ideas and his writings. The next article in the collection is 'Swinburne's Letters and Novels' (1962), which mentions his French background, and lingers on his admiration for Sade and his masochistic tendencies. There is, of course, much else in this essay on Swinburne besides the discussion of his desire for flagellation. Yet the topic is important to Wilson. From the days of his first European diary when he was intrigued by the torture-machines in the Nuremberg Tower (1908), to his last articles, he was interested in torture, and noticed sadistic or masochistic tendencies in a great variety of writers as different as Ben Jonson, Dickens, Dostoevsky, Lautréamont, Kipling, Mirbeau, Nabokov and Solzhenitsyn. 'It is a serious misrepresentation of Marx', he writes in *To the Finland Station*, 'to minimize the sadistic elements in his writing.' It provides him with an explanation not just of individual character but also of collective character. We should not ignore the fact that 'lust for cruelty' and 'appetite for destruction' are forces present throughout nineteenth-century literature, and have had a clear influence on the political events of this century. Wilson finds confirmation of his own views on this subject in the work of Mario Praz, especially *The Romantic Agony*, the theme of which is 'the development from the eighteenth century on, largely under the influence of the Marquis de Sade, of a literary tradition of erotic cruelty, hysterical enjoyment of horror and perverse admiration for crime' (1952, *The Bit Between My Teeth*, 1965). This book of Praz's is, I feel, one which Wilson would have liked to write himself, a wide-ranging comparative study of literature, especially French literature of the nineteenth century, linked by a theme which exercised his mind and sensibilities; it forms a clear and precise connection between *Axel's Castle* and *To the Finland Station*. Sade is in fact the writer who exemplifies most nearly the relation between revolutionary ideals and those of the symbolists at the end of the century.

The only other French writer to engage Wilson's attention in more than a desultory way was Flaubert, on whom there is an essay ('The Politics of Flaubert') in *The Triple Thinkers*. In spite of Flaubert's reputation for being interested only in his art and not at all in moral or social questions, Wilson sees him as being close to the historians Michelet, Renan and Taine. He takes a political standpoint against the socialists, disliking their materialism and authoritarianism, and preferring justice to equality. In those of his novels which are set in modern times (*Madame Bovary* and *L'Education sentimentale*) rather than in classical or christian times, there is a definite social comment which should not be minimized. The latter book, with its description of the Revolution of 1848, is to be compared with Marx's *Eighteenth Brumaire*. Flaubert's moral aims turn out to be very similar to those of Marx, and their im-implacable hatred of the bourgeois was something they had in common. The difference between them is this, that Flaubert thought it inevitable that socialists should turn into policemen, and Marx thought this was the fault of the bourgeois. The article concludes with an account of Flaubert's reaction to the Commune; he turned into an authoritarian and an elitist, like Saint-Simon whom he had earlier scorned. His disgust and disillusion appear in the disastrous play *Le Candidat* and even more so in *Bouvard et Pécuchet*. This essay on Flaubert is a good example of the way Wilson managed to present a complex subject, much debated by professional scholars, with clarity and simplicity, and yet with accuracy and control; it is also an example of his treating side by side the literature and the social thought of the nineteenth century.

There are one or two more French writers who momentarily aroused his interest. Anatole France is a special case. We have already seen the role he plays in *Axel's Castle* and in *To the Finland Station*. Now in spite of the criticism of him as a historian, Wilson never lost his affection for him. We shall see in a moment how he first discovered France's novels, but it is worth asking why it was that he continued to like him so much. As a writer Anatole France is still underrated today, in spite of some weighty French re-valuations of him, and it is as a writer that he appeals to Wilson. We can also see that France's personal blend of irony and lucidity was very close to Wilson's own. In *Le Jardin d'Epicure* which Wilson was familiar with, we read 'Plus je songe à la vie humaine, plus je crois qu'il faut lui donner pour témoins et pour juges l'Ironie et la Pitié'; this detachment and this compassion resulted from France's clear understanding of what men are like, and they were qualities which Wilson shared. In the same book France writes 'Une chose surtout donne de l'attrait à la pensée des hommes: c'est l'inquiétude. Un esprit qui n'est point anxieux m'irrite ou m'ennuie.' This too was something Wilson shared. France was not as ready as Wilson to see decadence and decline in literature and civilization; Wilson saw him as the last writer in the great French classical tradition, but perhaps France was right in saying that changes in civilization are in the long run smaller than one imagines. Another writer whom Wilson discovered at the same time as he did Anatole France was Octave Mirbeau. In *Classics and Commercials* there is an article 'In Memory of Octave Mirbeau' which first appeared in the *New Yorker* in 1949, in which he admits to the occasional nature of his interest in this minor and almost forgotten writer; he praises his vigorous and forthright journalism (like France he was active in the Dreyfus affair), and comments that his *Jardin des Supplices* contains 'the slightly cracked fairy-tales of a not ungenial old romantic who was still naive enough not to take such things for granted'. His liking for Anatole France was much less elegiac and nostalgic and lasted well over fifty years.

In 'Jean-Paul Sartre: the Novelist and the Existentialist' (1947, *Classics and Commercials*, 1950) Wilson acknowledges Sartre's gifts of invention and his public-spiritedness, but does not think that he is great. One can disagree with Wilson's supposition that *Morts sans Sépulture* was his best play so far (*Huis Clos* and *Les Mouches* being perhaps more promising contenders for the title) and accept his strictures on its rhetoric and lack of relation to experience. Existentialism, we are not surprised to learn, does not in the least attract him; he is happy simply to leave on one side its philosophical bases. In discussing Sartre's imaginary debate with a Marxist he awards the victory to the Marxist, though he finds Sartre more sincere and congenial than Soviet Marxists of the time. What he likes best in Sartre is his journalism in *Les Temps modernes*, for example the reflective irony of the *Portrait of an Anti-Semite*, which he likens to the work of the eighteenth-century Encyclopedists. He concludes that Sartre, bourgeois and provincial that he is, has qualities of industry, outspoken commonsense and a 'prosaic intelligence'. He is finally dismissed in these words: 'This does not, perhaps, necessarily make Sartre a top-flight writer, but, in these articles of *Les Temps modernes*, it does provide some very good reading.'

There are finally a few writers he mentions in passing, in essays which are about something else. The essay on 'The Sanctity of Baudelaire' (1947, *Classics and Commercials*, 1950) is really an attack on Eliot, Auden and Isherwood. Very often his passing remarks are disparaging references to people who irritate him. 'Sartre', he writes, 'is quite uninfected by the Cocteau-esque Parisian chichi of the interval between the wars', and in the whimsical 'An Interview with Edmund Wilson' (1962, *The Bit Between My Teeth*, 1965) he mentions Anouilh; the interviewer is made to intervene 'You don't care for Anouilh's plays?' and Wilson makes the following reply:

I abominate them. It's a kind of fraudulent cleverness that I hate to see them getting in France: forced whimsey – the French should never be whimsical – implausible improvised shocks, interminable *tirades* that pretend to mean something. Other people are doing it, too – Françoise Sagan, for example. Jean Cocteau began it when he became meretricious in his later plays; Giraudoux carried it on. Anouilh made an industry of it, and now his plays are being done everywhere – in England, America and Germany as well as in France. Yes, one of the chief problems of modern life is to avoid seeing Anouilh's plays.

Even when we allow for the intentionally provocative and frivolously exasperated nature of this outburst, we can see through the petulant and dyspeptic impatience to a very deep dissatisfaction.

This then is more or less the sum of the French writers mentioned by Wilson. Nothing much can be said about writers he may have read but never mentions. It is plain, however, that his reading of French literature, for all it was broad, was highly selective. French medieval literature is completely absent (the middle ages were not congenial to him – even Dante, whom he admires, stands outside his time), and he has not much to say about the writers of the Renaissance. This is strange, for Wilson has close affinities with the spirit of later Renaissance humanism, and there are some writers of that time whom he would have found congenial. Rabelais already has many of the popular, social attitudes he admires in the writers of the nineteenth century, yet he is scarcely named at all. Montaigne, too, is almost entirely absent, and this is odd, because his detached, enlighted commonsense and observation exactly matched Wilson's own. Montaigne is, I feel, the French writer he most closely

75

resembles, both temperamentally and stylistically. The classical writers and those of the eighteenth century are also missing in spite of his respect for the classical tradition and for rationalism. He leaves aside the Catholic tradition in French literature; in 1963 he made an effort to read Claudel's *Soulier de satin* but managed to get through only half of it. 'There are occasional gleams of poetry', he wrote, 'but the combination of rhetoric and religiosity, the supersexual and antisexual idealism that seems so effortful and not quite sincere, was rejected by my literary stomach', and elsewhere he does once refer to the egregious Teilhard de Chardin. One last absentee is Camus, whose ideas and style so often coincide with those of Wilson.

★   ★   ★

I want now to try to explain the origins and development of Wilson's active interest in France and her literature, and show how this sympathetic involvement gradually changed to a distant, detached and even cynical disillusionment. There is no need to dwell on the visits he made to France before the first war. He came to Europe as early as 1908 at the age of thirteen, and although the skimpy diary he kept during this period has been published (in *A Prelude*, 1967) it contains almost nothing on France, since he stopped keeping it in Paris. 'There is very little fun in Paris for children from other countries' he wrote about this in 1967. Yet this first trip and subsequent ones in the last splendid decaying years of the Edwardian era opened his mind and senses to the presence of old Europe, and allowed him to take its existence for granted. These early visits and the awareness of Europe they gave him were an encouragement and a stimulation, enabling him, when he went to Princeton in 1913, to profit from the inspired teaching of Christian Gauss. Wilson, like John Peale Bishop and Scott Fitzgerald, liked to talk about Gauss. The warm dedication of *Axel's Castle* tells what the book owes to his lectures of fifteen years previously, and the memorial to him in *The Shores of Light* (1952) recalls in particular his lectures on Flaubert and Dante ('a secular Dante – or rather, perhaps, a Dante of the Reformation'), and his passion for social and political thought. Gauss strengthened and clarified Wilson's young perceptions of France, helped to form his critical manners and method, and supported him with 'kindness and instruction' long after he left Princeton.

Wilson happened to be in London on the outbreak of war in 1914, but went back to America as quickly as he could. He returned to Europe in November 1917, and remained for over a year and a half in France, until July 1919, first in the Vosges, near Nancy, as a private in the Hospital Corps, and then at Chaumont in the Intelligence Corps. ('I enlisted in the hospital unit', he writes in *A Piece of My Mind*, 1956, 'in order not to wait for the draft and because it would not involve fighting.') This prolonged stay in provincial France in the special circumstances of the war affected him deeply. He says himself that he had already been 'something of a Francophile and ready to accept any Frenchman', and that because of this stay abroad he was able better to understand both foreigners, and Americans from different European origins. It gave him the opportunity, too, to read deeply, if not widely and with discrimination, in French literature. The choice was limited to what was available in wartime in a small country town. I am reminded of Daisy and Pete in *I Thought of Daisy* sitting round the fire reading aloud all Bulwer-Lytton's novels, because he was the only novelist available in the village library. Wilson has given us a list of the books he read at this time. His favourite was Anatole France with seventeen titles, followed by Octave Mirbeau with eight. The war also made him depressed, not just about war itself but about France and the French countryside. The first sign of this comes in *The Death of a Soldier*, a short story he wrote in the army which, because of censorship, he was not able to publish until after the war:

> France revealed itself as a gray and desolate country, where everything was either marsh or mud. The towns were all miserable-looking and exactly alike: dull red roofs and yellow walls, with washed-out streets between. The country consisted mostly of barren fields and dismal woods, inhabited by unfamiliar birds and there were endless lines of poplar skeletons in whose fishbone-like branches the mistletoe clumps were lodged like enormous nests. And everything was wet,

saturated with fog and rain. The men themselves were wet. It had been at least a week since they had been really dry. So this was Europe.

This fictional description, it seems to me, corresponds to the physical France which Wilson was to remember in later life.

It was immediately after the Armistice that he made what he called his 'first extended visit to Paris'. In 1921 he was in France again, arriving in Paris in late June. Leon Edel suggests that this trip 'seems to have been motivated by a desire to see Miss Millay, then abroad' (*The Twenties*, p. 36) and Wilson himself in his *Notebooks from a European Diary* (1963-4) published in the 1966 edition of *Europe Without Baedeker* recalls this period of his 'first great love'. After this there is an enormous gap in time before he came to stay in Europe again. During the rest of the twenties and thirties, the period when he was devoting so much energy to reading and writing about French symbolism, and French social thought, he did not set foot in France at all, except in 1935 when he passed through it on his way back from Russia. We may wonder how he resisted the temptation to cross the Atlantic at a time when so many of his contemporaries, writers and artists he knew well, went to settle in Paris, and create a new sort of social life in the cafés of Montparnasse. Is the answer that he already knew Paris well, and so found it less exciting than they did? Perhaps he was already aware that the glamorous dream it offered was an adolescent one, and had seen through the raffish sophistication of 'le frivole Paris illuminé', to borrow a phrase from Villiers de l'Isle-Adam, and perhaps he did not like the idea of belonging to a foreign intelligentsia. There is another reason which is more certain: he had by this time grown out of the faith in Europe which he had possessed as a young man.

It is true that after this he made several more trips to Europe but he was always disappointed. In 1945 he worked as a war correspondent for the *New Yorker* in England, Italy and Greece. The book which resulted from this trip, *Europe Without Baedeker* (with its subtitle 'Sketches Among the Ruins of Italy, Greece and England'), has little to say about France; its subject is the physical decay of Europe after the war, and the loss of spirit and energy

78

among the inhabitants. Europe, he was to write later, was at this time 'battered and grisly, demoralized'. Nine years after the war things were much the same: 'I had thought I should be glad to see France in February 1954, when I arrived at Calais from England, but, looking out of the window of the boat train in the late winter afternoon, I was seized by a sharp irritation.' Life was indeed better than in 1945, but in spite of his enormously enjoying 'the moderately priced champagne and the crisp and salty *pommes de terre frites* in the Café Voltaire' (which naggingly call to my mind 'the blown-up potatoes called *pommes de terre soufflées* of the delightful restaurant in the Rue de Rivoli' of 1908, remembered both in 1956 and 1967), Paris bores him as much as it did his six-year-old daughter. An unfortunate film of Sacha Guitry as Louis XIV (*Si Versailles m'était conté*) elicits the tart comment, 'Well, here was our poor dear old Europe self-consciously strutting her stuff.' He admits, however, in 1956 to feeling at sixty 'a certain yearning for London, Paris and Rome', and came to Europe in the summer of that year. The following spring, while he was at Talcottville he was once again nostalgic for London and Paris. 'The point is', he explains in *Upstate*, 'that – except for Talcottville – it is only in London and Paris that I can find, more or less unchanged, the things that I knew in my youth.' He was pleased that the familiar streets and buildings were still there and he had not stayed long enough to become aware of social and political changes. 'I am beginning to feel again about Paris' he adds 'the truth of all the clichés that, since my Francophile phase have annoyed me: "gracious living", "respect for literature", etc.' In 1962, in the interview I have already spoken about, he made the flippant remark 'I feel sometimes that I'm getting to the proverbial point when good Americans die and go to Paris. But of course if one went there alive, one might be killed by a plastic bomb. And then there are Anouilh's plays.' He did return to Europe in the following year, to stay in Paris, Rome and Budapest and, although in Paris he managed to avoid both the bombs and Anouilh's plays, his nostalgia did not survive the irritation and rigours of daily life there. The section on Paris in *Notes from a European Diary* is headed 'The Decline of Glamour'. The city had lost any tragic interest which the depredations of war had given it on earlier visits, having become Americanized, commonplace, provincial. Wilson talks almost regretfully of the abolition of the urinals, and the disappearance of the prostitutes, as well as of pretty well-dressed women, from the streets. He notices a dreariness and a lack of enthusiasm for the anachronistic De Gaulle. Here the observant tourist gives way to the sharp social commentator. Wilson senses an atmosphere of official repression, brought on by the Algerian troubles, which he has never before felt in Paris: Parisians talking in cafés are afraid of being overheard. He detects also a new attitude of the young towards the old, and sees the significance of recent student unrest, concluding the article on Paris like this: 'This winter a student riot, caused by the overcrowded classrooms and the deficient equipment of the Sorbonne, was broken up by police clubbings.'

In order to understand the change in Wilson's attitude to France and Europe it is necessary to consider what he saw as the relationship between Europe and America. I have said that his contact with Europe broadened his outlook, but this did not mean that he ever wanted to try to turn himself into a European. One of the elements which he most admired in American civilization was the union or federation of so many large states linked and preserved in relative harmony by a common language and culture. Europe, on the other hand, split into a multitude of small nations, divided from each other by their differences of language and culture, was always prone to war. During peacetime he deplored 'wrong-headed' nationalist revivals, and the revival or encouragement of minor national languages such as Gaelic, Landsmål and Romansh. Modern Hebrew, he agreed, was a regrettable necessity. Wilson was, of course, able to indulge his own nationalistic feelings because he happened to belong to a large nation; he himself was on occasion guilty of the sort of impatient prejudice which he disliked in Europeans. He had almost no knowledge of German and never thought it worth acquiring. This together with his consequent neglect of German ideas and German literature, may partly explain his anti-German attitude. He did spend a certain amount of time in Italy, but he was not really concerned with Italian literature, with the exception of Dante whom he knew well, and odd writers he happened to come across, such as Silone and Moravia. He regrets his lack of Portuguese and Spanish. Spain represents, in fact, a curious blockage for him. This is expressed with almost unbelievable plainness in 'The Genie of the Via Giulia' (1965, *The Bit Between My Teeth*, 1965):

> I, too, like Mario Praz – as he explains in a new edition [of *The Romantic Agony*] of 1954 – have been bored by Hispano-philes, and I have also been bored by everything, with the exception of Spanish painting, that I have ever known about Spain. I have made a point of learning no Spanish, and I have never got through *Don Quixote*; I have never visited Spain or any other Hispanic country. But Mario Praz does know Spanish and *has* visited Spain, and his report on it confirms me in my prejudices.

It is not a sufficient answer to this to say that it is journalism, hasty generalization or tongue-in-cheek aside. I think he means it. It does, however, put into perspective his attitude to France and French literature; it also shows that the Europe which attracted and repelled him was not even the whole of Europe. Most of Europe he was not remotely interested in. Yet there remains his concern for a comparative study of literature, long before this became fashionable. In 'A Modest Self-Tribute' (1952, *The Bit Between My Teeth*, 1965) he claims that he has tried to contribute to the 'general cross-fertilization', establishing relationships between American and European cultures and between those of different European countries. If the limitations can be allowed for, he is certainly successful in this.

Wilson's negative, sometimes even hostile, attitude to Europe goes a long way towards explaining his theory of 'isolationism' during the wars. In *A Piece of My Mind* he criticizes America's involving herself in European war:

> In 1917 we had been saving Europe from the Germans; in the forties we had been saving it from the Germans again; we shall presently be returning no doubt – unless our mentality changes – to rescue it from the Russians. But the more we save Europe from the Huns and the Goths, the more wretched she

seems to get. Was she really proud and splendid in our youth? How demoralized France became at the end of the first of these wars; how depraved and macabre the whole continent at the end of the second one; how far gone in decomposition seem so many things one sees there today! How futile to try to save Europe, who does nothing to save herself.

He returns so often to this subject of decline, collapse and imminent disintegration, that it appears as an obsession, a real fear, mixed with complacency and even delight, and not just something he 'picked up in the Ritz bar in Paris' (*I Thought of Daisy*). Europe has already reached the position where its assumptions of cultural supremacy are no longer warranted. In *A Piece of My Mind* we find the following *boutade*:

A certain kind of European overrates the comparative importance in the present age of the world, of a good deal of his cultural tradition, and often of his own real interest in it. For myself, as an American, I have not the least doubt that I have derived a good deal more benefit of the civilizing as well as of the inspirational kind from the admirable American bathroom than I have from the cathedrals of Europe.

Cathedrals, he admits, are beautiful and can be useful (in the past for prayer, today for shelter on a hot day) but American culture has now superseded European, even though so many European refugees in America complain of a lack of culture there. Wilson's mind on the subject is laid bare in a quotation he gives from Gibbon's *Decline and Fall* which declares that if there were to be new barbarian invasions in Europe, then 'ten thousand vessels would transport beyond their pursuit the remains of civilized society; and Europe would revive and flourish in the American world, which is already filled with her colonies and institutions'. Writing in 1929 of the similarity between the situation of America and that of Russia with respect to Western Europe ('Dostoevsky Abroad' in *The Shores of Light*) he points to the permanent difficulty for America of adapting European culture to her own. What is new since the first war – and this disturbs him profoundly – is that America has been importing European gloom ('the emotions and the points of view appropriate to bankruptcy and exhaustion – resignation, futility and despair') into a prosperous, forward-looking country.

Not only did Wilson himself not settle in Europe in the twenties, but he was disappointed that others did so. Of Thornton Wilder he wrote in 1928 'Mr. Wilder already knows Europe, and he also knows something of the Orient; and now we need him at home' (*Shores of Light*), and of John Peale Bishop who was in Europe from 1922 to 1924 and from 1927 to 1933 he said in 1948 that in the early twenties 'one regretted his absence from America, where one imagined that the literary revival would have continued to be stimulating for him' (*The Collected Essays of John Peale Bishop*). In 1921, just before Wilson had left for Europe Scott Fitzgerald wrote to him from London:

> God damn the continent of Europe. It is of merely antiquarian interest. . . . France made me sick. Its silly pose as the thing the world has to save. I think it's a shame that England and America didn't let Germany conquer Europe. . . . When Anatole France dies French literature will be a silly jealous rehashing of technical quarrels. They're thru and done. You may have spoken in jest about New York as the capital of culture but in 25 years it will be just as London is now. (*Letters*, ed. Andrew Turnbull, p. 326)

Fitzgerald's coat-trailing remarks here are a clear reflection of Wilson's own ideas, and when Wilson spoke about New York as the capital of culture it was not in jest. He strongly wished to shift the centre of the literary world away from Paris and London. I am reminded that French writers in the Renaissance were fond of saying that literature and the arts had travelled first from Athens to Rome and then from Rome to Paris (sometimes grudgingly admitting that Florence had been a stage on the way); Wilson seems to be saying that after the decline and fall of Paris there has been a similar *translatio litterarum* to New York. In 'A dissenting opinion on Kafka' (1947, *Classics and Commercials*, 1950), although he does not like Kafka and finds the adulation of him disconcerting, he is proud to be able to record that a new collected edition 'of a modern

83

German classic, which was begun in Berlin under Hitler and only finished in Prague on the eve of the German occupation of Czechoslovakia, should thus have been salvaged from the ruins of Central European culture and brought out in the United States'. This may, I think, be taken as a symbol of the transference of culture from the old world to the new. To return to Gibbon's image, America will welcome European men of letters and artists when the barbarians force them to the boats – as she in fact did – and literature will be born again in the west. But, as in the case of Rome, Florence and Paris, this is possible only because of the already existing American culture.

A few words in conclusion. I come back again to the comparison with Montaigne. The only comments Wilson makes about Montaigne, as far as I recall, refer to his scepticism and his garrulousness. Wilson, too, is sceptical, and, yes, garrulous at times. But the talk is good, and like Montaigne's it will last. His critical journalism records his daily reflections, sometimes rambling, but round rather than away from the point, much in the manner of the *Essais*. In neither his case nor Montaigne's could anyone call the result ephemeral; Wilson's prose is classical, in the sense he applied the term to Anatole France. There were times, especially in later life, when Wilson felt isolated from his own century, and that the life he led was not very different from that of a man of the eighteenth century. He shared Montaigne's desire for isolation and seclusion. Montaigne retreated to his château at Montaigne, with the round tower in which he made his library. Wilson, of course, had no such refuge (unless it were Talcottville or perhaps a room in snowy Cambridge, Massachusetts) but it is curious to notice how often he returns to the image of the castle or stronghold. In neither his case nor Montaigne's was this seclusion in any sense monastic. Montaigne, as well as being a sociable country gentleman, was a diplomatic agent and was twice mayor of Bordeaux; Wilson was always closely concerned with the cultural life of his society, and an enthusiastic and impassioned supporter of the successive causes he took up. His interest in French Symbolism, French social and revolutionary thought, and a new French humanism, was, as I have tried to show, deeply felt and energetically pursued. But it was one interest among many and it is not surprising that it gradually gave place to others.

I have spoken of Edmund Wilson and France. What of France and Edmund Wilson? Here there is not much to say. Three of his books have been translated into French: *To the Finland Station* by Georgette Camille in 1965, *Memoirs of Hecate County* by Bruno Vercier in 1966, and *I Thought of Daisy* by Michel Doury, with an embarrassingly glib introduction, in 1969. I do not think that they have made much impact, though I like to think that *To the Finland Station* played some part in the events of May 1968. Why is it that *Axel's Castle* has not been translated? (I could not even find a copy of it in the Bibliothèque nationale, that stronghold whose bureaucratic inefficiency had so depressed Wilson.) One reason is that French people are generally not aware of what foreigners write about their literature and, when they are aware, cannot be expected to like it when the criticism is adverse and the idols are unseated; another reason is that neither the thirties nor the forties were propitious moments for literary criticism which was not politically motivated, and by the fifties Wilson's positions were taken for granted. But it is a pity.

There have already been American dissertations on Wilson, who was a lifelong railer against academics; some day, no doubt, he will receive the ultimate accolade of a monumental French thesis for the Doctorat d'Etat.

HELEN MUCHNIC

Edmund Wilson's Russian Involvement

I

Edmund Wilson's fascination with Russia began when he was a university student and lasted to the end of his life. It involved his major interests – literary, linguistic, religious, philosophic; touched off a variety of conflicting emotions; and provoked some of his finest writing.

It was probably Christian Gauss of Princeton who introduced him, among other great literatures, to the Russian – Christian Gauss, to whom Wilson paid tribute, first, in his dedication to him of *Axel's Castle*, then, in the essay that stands as Prologue to *The Shores of Light*, 'Christian Gauss as a Teacher of Literature'. In both of these, a gifted pupil addresses with devoted gratitude the master who has enlightened and inspired him; and, if one considers Wilson's writing with these tributes in mind, one becomes aware of how profoundly the precepts and skills of the admired teacher were imprinted on his pupil's mind. Not the least of these was an ability to recognize and honor artistic greatness beyond the frontiers of nationality and the barriers of language. Gauss would point, for example, to Dante's superiority over Shakespeare and of Flaubert's over English novelists in the matter of objectivity. 'He admired the Russians also', Wilson recalled, 'for their sober art of implication. I remember his calling our attention to one of the church scenes in Tolstoy's *Resurrection*, in which, as he pointed out, Tolstoy made no overt comment, yet caused you to loathe the whole thing by describing the ceremony step by step. This non-English, this classical and Latin ideal, became indissolubly associated in our minds with the summits of literature.' Thus, early in his career,

Wilson perceived Tolstoy's genius to be of the same order as Dante's and Flaubert's, the genius of precise observation intensely experienced, its full meaning implicit in the overt statement.

This also was the time when Wilson became acquainted with Dostoevsky. In *A Prelude* he speaks of how, having read *The Brothers Karamazov* 'with enthusiasm', he sent it to his friend Alfred Bellinger, with whom he had agreed to exchange books every Christmas, so that each of them would read a work the other had enjoyed and that he might otherwise have missed. But Alfred did not like *The Brothers Karamazov*. 'Why, there's not a Christian character in the book!' he said, which made Edmund 'take account of the chasm between Alfred's Congregationalism and Dostoevsky's Slavic Christianity', the first of many instances when he was forced to take account of chasms that yawned between America and Russia.

After Princeton, Wilson lived for a while in Greenwich Village and worked as a reporter for the New York *Evening Sun*. Then war intervened. He enlisted in a hospital unit and spent almost two years in the army. No titles of Russian books appear in the long list he kept of his reading during these tiresome and distressing months. But a story of the time, 'The Death of a Soldier', seems to me to be strikingly Tolstoyan. When he republished it in *A Prelude*, Wilson said in a prefatory note that it described a real case and that 'most of the incidents' in it were also real. So too were the characters and incidents in Tolstoy's early tales of army life. And, whether Wilson was already familiar with these or not, his story reveals a strongly similar outlook: a subdued realism, abhorrence of human callousness, pity for the remorseless waste of a young life. The bitter irony implicit in the matter-of-fact conclusion, ' "He put up a pretty good fight there at the last", remarked the doctor, noting the death in a register . . . ', is very like Tolstoy's. Another story, 'Lieutenant Franklin', is also Tolstoyan in its emphasis on the unnaturalness of war that disrupts ordinary human concerns and thwarts the mutual interests and normal friendliness of people by forcing them to be enemies.

When he was mustered out and returned to New York in July 1919, Wilson was filled with a sense of tremendous relief and

D   87

complete liberation not only from the onerous duty of military service, although the nightmare of war was never to be forgotten, but also from the social and family traditions which he had hitherto taken for granted. In the dull, uncomfortable and horrible period of service, he had had 'leisure to think', and his thoughts, combined with army friendships 'with all kinds of people' made him realize that the world he had lived in was not his world, that he had 'never quite believed' in it, 'had never, in fact, quite belonged to it'. 'It suddenly became very clear to me that I could never go back to my former life – that is, that I could never go back to the habits and standards of even the most cultivated elements of the world in which I lived. . . . It now appeared to me too narrowly limited by its governing principles and prejudices. My experience of the army had had on me a liberating effect.' He now plunged with relish into the new post-war life of 'the jazz age', and soon became one of its most brilliant spokesmen. His record of it is abundant and many-sided. Its idealism and rebelliousness, its wild gaiety and its tragedy are pictured in his diaries and notebooks, his novel, his plays, his reviews of all the arts – drama, cinema, art, music, his reports of court proceedings and grim occurrences on city streets: pitiful and sordid trials, defenceless people victimized by crass injustice, lovely parks and fine buildings ruined or destroyed through fatal indifference.

Russia entered the consciousness of this active but unlovely world in the aspect not only of literature but, increasingly, of social philosophy and politics. Dostoevsky and Chekhov were in vogue and, although Wilson did not succumb to fashionable adulation, he wrote of them with appreciativeness and originality, while events in Russia led him to a study of socialism and Karl Marx.

The Moscow Art Theater came to New York in 1923. Wilson recognized in its performance the quality he had already learned to admire. Its realism, he wrote, which belonged not to the Naturalistic school of Zola, Arnold Bennett and Dreiser but to that of Flaubert, Turgenev, Henry James and Anatole France, 'went beyond notation, beyond merely reproducing the surface of life'. It recreated 'the beauty and poignancy of an atmosphere, of an idea, a person, a moment . . . without emphasis, without anything which we recognize as theatrical, but with the brightness of the highest art'. In *The Cherry Orchard*, it presented 'with impressive exactitude' not only 'a complex of social relations' but also 'the charm about this Russian gentry . . . in such a way that their futility is moving, their ineptitude touched with the tragedy of every human failure'. Many years later, as he began to reconstruct his life, Wilson remembered that, when he saw this production, he was teased by an awareness of something vaguely familiar, and then realized that Chekhov's picture of old-time Russia was not unlike what he himself had seen in childhood in his Aunt Caroline's home in New Jersey: 'the same spirit of family cohesiveness, the same amiable frivolity and futility'. He sensed, that is, on a deeply personal level, a kinship between these Russians, far removed in time and space, and his own intimate American background, while the art of the Moscow theater appealed to his taste for the kind of unrhetorical under-statement that, without distorting reality, was able to convey it with exquisite poignancy. What if their beautiful performance, even of Gorky's *The Lower Depths*, was too smooth to do justice to the violence of the world? This was as it should be; it was 'inevitable for this form of art to eliminate the surprising and the violent. There are no earthquakes in Henry James; and in Flaubert – in his fiction, at least, which deals with contemporary subjects – even a revolution is never allowed to be shattering. This is the art of steady underemphasis and of effects that are slowly unfolded.'

When, three years later, the Moscow Art Theater returned to New York, Wilson seemed to contradict himself. He now praised their production of *Lysistrata* for its earthiness and crudeness, which, he said, combined with imaginative intelligence, were perfectly suited to Aristophanes, as our own productions could not be. He ascribed these newly found qualities to the distinctive character of the Russians, much as he ascribed *The Ziegfield Follies*, 'a glittering vision which (rose) straight out of the soul of New York', to the nature of Americans. The stiff and formal jokes, the uniform tempo corresponded exactly to the American taste for 'the efficiency of mechanical movement', an 'expression of nervous intensity to the tune of harsh and complicated harmonies', like the subway one took home after the performance that sped one to one's goal 'with a crash like a fast song by Eddie Cantor'. As Ziegfield was America, the Moscow Art Theater was Russia. Wilson found 'something harsh and unsympathetic' in Russian humor, in Chekhov's 'ferocious one-act farces' by comparison to his 'serious long plays'. But this 'shocking harshness' was characteristic also of the literature of ancient Greece, whose peculiar fascination, by contrast to modern literature and even to that of Rome, was 'the piquancy of a high culture still rooted in primitive traditions'. In modern times this combination of high culture and primitivism was possessed by the Russians alone. They were 'closer to the earth and further from the industrialized world than any other great Western people', and they had 'brought their theater to a perfection that (was) probably unique'. This was why 'only these actors from the barbarous steppe', fusing 'efficiency and intelligence with animal spirits and natural directness', could revive Greek plays in such a way that 'among the crowd of Athenian women' one could imagine catching 'a glimpse of the female greengrocer who gave birth to Euripides and the midwife who was Socrates' mother'.

Was it this performance, one wonders, which first suggested the idea that presently emerged as the crux of Wilson's artistic credo, and which, as his theory takes shape in these early years, crops up variously: in an article on Proust, that becomes part of *Axel's Castle*, in an article on Dostoevsky, incorporated into *I Thought of Daisy*, and in other pieces, to be ultimately defined in his celebrated essay on the *Philoctetes* of Sophocles? The idea, crudely summarized, is that, in the harmonious beauty of great art, the brutalities of life are incorporated in all their savage roughness and not omitted and smoothed over, as the school of Humanism, represented by Irving Babbitt and Paul Elmore Moore, chose to assume. In the late twenties, the Humanists were exercising considerable influence in academic circles. Wilson denounced with fury their moralizing misinterpretations of the Greeks. The 'moral philosophy' that they professed to derive from Sophocles, he wrote, seemed to him 'pure baloney'. How did they stand 'in regard to the nobility of matricide and in regard to all the other outrageous things for which the characters in Greek tragedies claim a divine sanction?' Great art, whether ancient or modern, was not a preaching of the good but a dramatization of man's experience. Its excellence depended on the artist's intensity, depth and completeness of perception, not on moralistic purposes, but on knowledge and understanding. This intensity, completeness and depth Wilson found in Dostoevsky as well as in Sophocles and Proust.

In his essay on Proust, he remarked that Dostoevsky was 'one of the most satisfactory novelists' from the point of view of 'completeness', which one also felt in Proust's world and which was not just 'the variety of elements' in it but the way these elements were made to compose 'an organic whole', and this depended on the close tie between the author and his creation. 'Myshkin and Rogozhin thrill us because they are the opposite poles of one nature; the three brothers Karamazov move us because they are the spirit, mind and body of one man.' In this respect 'even so great a novelist as Dickens' fell short of Dostoevsky, for he admitted into his novels a 'conventional element . . . "good" characters and villains into whom he scarcely projected himself at all'. A novelist's 'projecting himself' into his characters indicated that he understood the significance of what happened in the world and was fully conscious of his own relationship to it. It was by this criterion that Wilson judged the work not only of novelists but of all artists, and on this scale the Russians measured high.

'Meditations on Dostoevsky', published in the *New Republic* in 1928, is, I think, more passionate than any other of Wilson's writings. Its ardor reflected, no doubt, the headlong atmosphere of post-war society and his own emotional entanglements and personal tensions of all kinds; and he himself seems to have been dubious about its tone, seeking to temper its intensity in a disparaging subtitle, 'Bad Quarter-Hour of a Literary Critic', but that he set store by the article is shown in the way he used it in *I Thought of Daisy*, where, broken up to fit the plot and somewhat moderated, it is made to stand at the very core of the hero's philosophic reflections.

The problem suggested by Dostoevsky was the knotty problem of ethics and art, and specifically, of the bearing of the artist's life, when it was involved with the most unsavory aspects of human experience – disease, corruption, vice – on his imaginary creations.

'As Dostoevsky is one of the greatest modern writers, so he is also perhaps the one who may make us most discontented with literature', Wilson began. 'When one remembers his sadistic obsessions, his complaisance in self-degradation, his extravagant vanity, one begins to feel that the masterpieces of such a man of genius were only a doubtful compensation on paper for the misdeeds and defects of a life. Are not the purity of Dostoevsky's tenderness, the flights of his Christian idealism, to be measured precisely by the fierceness of his perversity, the subhuman depths of his indifference? Are not the Svidrigailovs and the Stavrogins . . . the price that one has to pay for the Alyoshas and Prince Myshkins?' These conventional questions he then showed up to be paltry misapprehensions, obtuse blindness to the complex and heroic nature of the artistic process. Dostoevsky who 'had been forced to live at the closest quarters, both within and without, with the basic contentions and discords, the basic horrifying anomalies of human life' had succeeded 'by heroic effort, an effort never relaxed' to redress 'the moral balance of that universe which he had once felt reeling about him with the world of his own soul'. Such was the artist's arduous and magnificent achievement. 'These contentions, anomalies and discords are they not the provokers of all important literature? . . . Is there, in fact, from the point of view of horror and barbarity, much to choose between Sophocles and Dostoevsky himself? . . . Are not Stavrogin's rape, Myshkin's epilepsy and Zossima's putrefaction, quite matched by Oedipus' incest, Philoctetes' ulcer and Polyneices' corpse?' Thirteen years later, in 'The Wound and the Bow', this argument received its most eloquent formulation, when Philoctetes, mentioned here in passing, became the touching, tragic symbol of artistic creation.

II

But intellectuals in the twenties were drawn to Russia also by interests that were not literary. Dissatisfied with their world and with themselves, they looked to Russia for solutions of their problems. Wilson's experience of this state of mind – a tangle of hope, despair, guilt, idealism – is recorded in nearly everything he wrote. *The Crime in the Whistler Room*, for example, first performed in 1924, and later described by him as 'a fantasy of our first liberation from the culture and convention of the previous era', is a satire on a complacent, unfeeling society, which ends romantically, in defiance of bourgeois tradition, with the union of a creative artist and an uneducated girl, symbolically, that is, with the union of art and the proletariat, the only representatives of genuine life in a dead world. A grim sketch, called 'Reunion', presents a nightmare view of post-war disillusionment with governments that cannot stop wars with men who, through the experience of military regimentation, have come to like dictatorship, with 'one's own fatal human inadequacy . . . one's possibilities for cowardice, for brutality, for bestiality'. It is a mood of hopelessness and cynicism, for 'To learn to think ill of oneself is to learn to think ill of the world'.

How cope with these horrors, with this sense of outrage to humanity and with one's own guilty complicity in this outrage? The hero of *I Thought of Daisy*, like Nat Graves of 'Reunion', feels that 'one could never go back now to living indifferently and trivially; one was afraid of lending oneself to some offense against that unhappy humanity which one shared with other men'. Beneath the hectic, pleasure-seeking surface of the jazz age, there lurked the memory of nightmare, guilt, terror, and the high resolve to conquer these by living in recognition of one's alliance with 'that unhappy humanity', whose destiny one shared.

The chance to test this alliance arrived dramatically with the Great Depression. Wilson all but abandoned his literary pursuits to observe the effects of the collapse and to examine its causes and consider possible remedies. 'From the fall of 1930 to the spring of 1934,' he wrote later, 'I spent a good deal of time reporting political and industrial events, and thereafter, till 1940, writing a study of Marxism and the Russian Revolution.' He travelled from coast to coast of the United States and sent in graphic, terse, profoundly moving reports of nation-wide suffering and bewilderment: of defiant protests and helpless struggle, of courageous but ineffectual strikes, of men and women numbed by despair, of pitiful suicides. He contemplated the sordid scene unsentimentally, and denounced the cruelty of a disorganized society that was 'a festering disgrace to humanity – with decent people turned into outlaws and sent to jail for demanding a living'. His picture of American democracy was of a 'machine' that 'has been running down . . . of a life which aims at nothing beyond itself, which is a part of no general human effort'.

His 'study of Marxism and the Russian Revolution' was, by contrast, the history of an ideal. He traced it from the eighteenth century to the twentieth, from Giovanni Vico's grasp of 'the *organic* character of human society and the importance of reintegrating through history the various forces and factors which actually compose human life', to the evolution of this concept, from Jules Michelet to Karl Marx, in the minds of philosophers and the experiments of sociologists and economists in the nineteenth century, to its potential realization in the Russian Revolution. He called his work *To the Finland Station*, using Lenin's arrival at this terminal on 16 April 1917 as the symbolic moment 'when for the first time in the human exploit the key of a philosophy of history was to fit an historical lock', for this was the moment when 'Western man' could be seen 'to have made some definite progress in mastering the greeds and the fears, the bewilderments, in which he has lived'. Disillusionment was to come. But as late as 1940 Wilson was still intoxicated with the grandeur of the idea he had traced, and still believed, even in the face of menacing portents, that, at long last, the great idea was attaining, in the revolutionary state of the Soviet Union, a much delayed, and often frustrated, application.

Thirty years later, in 1971, in the introduction to a new edition of *To the Finland Station*, he explained his error as an instance of the idealistic optimism that prevailed among liberals before they were confronted by the shattering reality of the Second World War and the revelations of Stalin's tyranny. 'It is all too easy', he wrote 'to idealize a social upheaval which takes place in some other country than one's own.' And just as Englishmen once idealized the French Revolution, and the French the American, so 'American socialists and liberals' idealized the Russian Revolution. 'The remoteness of Russia from the West evidently made it even easier . . . to imagine that the Russian Revolution was to get rid of an oppressive past, to scrap a commercial civilization and to found, as Trotsky prophesied, the first really human society. We were very naive about this.' Similarly, some years earlier, in 1958, in a Postscript that accompanied a collection of his reports on the Depression, *The American Earthquake*: 'All the radicals of that time like myself who were impressed by the efforts of the Soviet Union without any first-hand experience of Russia were bemused by a certain utopianism. . . . For me and for others like me, the Kremlin meant the Third International, and this meant the organization of the "workers of the world" to vindicate their human rights against everything we hated in contemporary society.'

III

In 1935 Wilson went to Russia. When, on the way, he saw England again, after eighteen years, he remembered how in 1917, 'at Southampton . . . in a rest-camp which was deep in water', he 'had read in the English papers little scraps about more trouble in Russia with men named Lenin and Trotsky coming to the top . . . and now I was returning to Europe with books about Lenin and a Russian grammar'. The Soviet boat was pleasant, his three young cabin mates extraordinarily considerate, and the general atmosphere, with 'the liquidation of social and radical distinctions', one of 'quiet amiability'. But the chairs were straight-backed and uncomfortable and were all screwed down so that no one could move them, which led him to remark: 'with all that is lax in Russia there is, as I was afterwards to find, always something of which the severity is terribly overdone'.

He spent five months in the Soviet Union; stayed in Leningrad and Moscow, voyaged down the Volga, stopping off at Ulyanovsk to visit Lenin's early home, which he described in *To the Finland Station*, then, by way of Stalingrad, Rostov-on-the Don, and Kiev, to Odessa, where having caught scarlet fever, he was incarcerated for six weeks in the Hospital for Contagious Diseases.

He had sailed under the impression, which he shared with his liberal friends at home, that the Soviet Union was 'simply the U.S. plus one's ideal of socialism' – a preconception that was quickly shaken. Time and again a tantalizing sense of the familiar would be blotted out by something utterly foreign: the strangeness of a scene, the puzzling behavior of the people. On board ship he had felt more at home with the Russians, whose language he did not know, than with his English fellow-passengers; Lenin's house was like one in New England; and it was 'much easier', he thought, 'to establish friendly relations with Russians than with the people of any other country' he knew. But the 'first impression of Leningrad' was 'of something completely unfamiliar'. It was 'absolutely dream-like and dazing'. Drably dressed people moved quietly in 'mute and monstrous hordes' through 'a town of wide boulevards' with 'enormous public buildings and palaces' that were oppressive and grisly. And in Moscow, which was surprisingly 'modern and energetic', people '(ripped) around the streets in their Russian-made cars, tooting wild defiant horns, like galloping Cossacks'. But in the Park of Culture and Rest, which seemed 'like limbo' to an American, they moved 'very slowly' with expressionless faces, neither laughing nor singing and seemed 'not even to talk to one another'. Were they sobered by hardship, Wilson wondered, or were they 'still . . . numb and dumb from their old subhuman serfdom?' Later, he was told by one of his Russian friends that, like everyone else, they were terribly afraid.

He was bothered, too, by the glorification of Stalin, whose photograph appeared on the front page of almost every newspaper and to whom a tribute was placed at the end of 'every speech and important public document . . . like the prayer at the end of a sermon'; but he tried to find excuses for this, and admonished his American readers to remember 'that before the Revolution, eighty per cent of the Russians were illiterate', that they were totally ignorant of democracy, that 'a paternalistic government' and a state of serfdom in which men 'were exchanged for pigs and dogs' had existed in their country for centuries. How could they, who had 'never seen any other newspapers', be expected 'to criticize the Soviet press?' But he was also baffled and annoyed by certain characteristics which, he decided, were basic in the Russian nature. The Russians were disorganized and unreliable, they preferred vagueness to punctuality, behaved unpredictably, and had no sense of time. At one point, in complete exasperation, he exclaimed:

'There are moments when the evasiveness, the procrastination, the imprecision and the meekness of the Russians bring out the Ivan the Terrible in all of us.'

His period of quarantine in the crowded and 'terribly dirty' hospital in Odessa, infested with bugs, swarming with flies, with garbage piled up in the bathrooms, confirmed his impression of Russian inefficiency, indecisiveness and carelessness. It also provided one of the most entertaining chapters in the whole literature of travel. His sketches of the exasperating, incompetent, officious, quarrelsome, warm-hearted, clumsy Russians – the nurses, the 'extremely attractive and extremely badly behaved' children, the Intourist interpreter, the representative from the Komsomol, the young bacteriological research worker – compose a striking gallery of portraits, more convincing and endearing, to my mind, than the personages of Wilson's fictions. The pictures unfold gradually, in sequence, as traits are revealed to the observer, and some of them, like the one of the hospital doctor, come to life, in the way Chekhov's often do, in hilarious episodes and poignant details that add up to a heartbreaking image of nobility and pathos.

On his last night in Leningrad, Wilson had attended a perform-ance of Tchaikovsky's opera, *The Queen of Spades*, in Meyerhold's production which skilfully underscored the sinister elements of the libretto. And his first impressions of Russia were summed up in a magnificent prose poem of mystery and desolation, in which Pushkin's terrifying tragedy blended with the setting of his room when he went to bed, 'full of vodka and Pushkin . . . a cut-glass decanter' on the table 'with a curious high square stopper and full of water that hadn't been changed for days', the sky 'still pale with unfading day . . . outside the high windows', and saw, with a clarity that obliterated the past, Pushkin's and Dostoevsky's characters moving through 'the vast sprawling city with the bottomless spaces behind it . . . the great unintegrated city . . . away there on the outskirts of Europe'. In this, he reflected, there was kinship between Russians and Americans, kinship in the precarious-ness of their existence, in uncertainty and hardship and the necessity of intense individual effort. For these people 'had come back as we had done at home to a strongly provincial civilization among prairies and wild rivers and forests, bringing books and manners from Europe'. 'In these countries,' he thought, 'we are freer, less certain of what we want, we think the long long thoughts of the poem and they are lost in the quiet of the province . . . unless, all alone in the spaces, we are possessed by some passionate purpose. . . . We never know what we have got in the forests and wastes of these countries; we never know what is going to come of them. . . .'

In 'Final Reflections', a brief chapter that closes the book, to which, twenty years later, he appended a long explanatory Post-script, Wilson wrote that, although one's first impressions of Russia were likely to be contradictory, once one got glimpses of what went on 'beneath the surface', one became aware of 'an extra-ordinary heroism'. One was made to feel, on every hand, 'the ter-rible seriousness of what (was) being done in Russia and the terrible cost it (entailed)'. Despite the defects of the regime, 'the lack of democratic procedure, the suppression of political opposition, the constraint of the official terror . . . you feel in the Soviet Union that you are living at the moral top of the world, where the light never really goes out . . .'. He concluded with a description of crowds at the tomb of Lenin, so glowing in praise of the idolized hero, that one cannot read it today without embarrassment.

He returned home in the fall of 1935. His Russian pieces, under the heading 'U.S.S.R. May – October 1935' were published the following year together with a group of articles, called 'U.S.A. November 1932 – May 1934' – most of them had already appeared in the *New Republic* – in a book, the title of which, *Travels in Two Democracies*, indicates the angle of his approach to the Soviet Union. Its 'Epilogue' deserves to be quoted in full, especially since it has not been reprinted, because it is as eloquent a statement as one can find of Edmund Wilson's *profession de foi*. His feeling for the 'two democracies', with their great aims and their terrible shortcomings, with the native similarities and differences of their people, impelled him to emphasize his belief that human destiny was shaped by human beings, and that, despite their readiness to abdicate authority and responsibility, man's fate rested not in the lap of the gods but in the hands of individuals; the power was theirs, and thence also, the duty:

98

THE TRAVELLER. The factories, the committee rooms, the parades; the amusement parks, the meeting halls, the bars – they are as empty as I myself when I go into them. Seen so, the life of men can give them nothing: they have no other life than I. He who said, 'in His will is our peace', – it was with his own will that he was reconciled; he who said, 'Lord, forgive them!' – it was he himself who had forgiven. And so he who first saw and said that man advanced on his belly – he himself had risen upright; and he who spoke in the name of the masses – it was he who gave them their soul. The states slip; the people cringe; all look after vanishing suns. Yet still we refer to obsolete authorities decisions which must be made by ourselves, yet still we invoke from invisible forces the power we ourselves do not find. Still we think in terms of mythologies in this day when, if God cannot help us, the People or the Masses can do no better – when accuracy of insight, when courage of judgement, are worth all the names in all the books.

IV

After he came back from the Soviet Union, Wilson continued to study Russian. He enjoyed it prodigiously, and was soon to write even of the monstrous difficulties of its grammar with such entrancing delight and of the rewards it offered with such tempting promises of pleasure, that only the laziest of language students could have resisted his blandishments. Among the greatest of the rewards was Pushkin, the magic of whose verse was a revelation to Wilson when he read him in the original. He wrote on him repeatedly, the first time in 1937 for the centenary of his death, in articles that inaugurated a series of essays on Russian writers that were to appear over the next thirty years. Some of them were included in *Classics and Commercials, The Shores of Light, The Triple Thinkers* and *The Bit Between My Teeth*. Finally, in *A Window on Russia*, Wilson gathered up 'all the pieces on Russian subjects that I have not collected in other volumes'. It came out in 1972, the year of his death.

His first piece on Pushkin, on *Evgenii Onegin*, showed his skill in

99

bringing a foreign poet home to his readers by introducing him in the company of those they already knew. He found the means of giving an idea of Pushkin's quality by first contrasting his conciseness and meticulous workmanship with Byron's prolixity and laxness, to correct the usual misconception that Pushkin was a Russian Byron; then, he compared him to Keats. Setting side by side a passage from 'The Eve of Saint Agnes' and a comparable one from *Evgenii Onegin*, which he offered in a literal translation, he exhorted the reader to imagine it 'done in something like Keats's marrowy line'. Pushkin, he noted, 'can make us see and hear things as Keats can, but his range is very much greater'. He illustrated the extent and variety of this range, and remarked that Pushkin had never been surpassed, not even by Tennyson in *In Memoriam* nor Baudelaire in *Les Fleurs du Mal* in 'making poetry of classical firmness and precision out of a world realistically observed.' In passing, he suggested that Pushkin may have been influenced by Praed, whose *The Vicar* was closer to *Evgenii Onegin* than *Don Juan*; and he summed up the uniqueness of *Evgenii Onegin* in Western literature as follows: 'To have written a novel in verse, and a novel of contemporary manners, which was also a great poem, was Pushkin's unprecedented feat – a feat which, though several times attempted by later poets of the nineteenth century, was never to be repeated.' As for the character of the hero, Onegin differed from the romantic creations of Byron, Chateaubriand and even Lermontov, and was comparable only to Stendhal's Julien Sorel, so that this great novel in verse 'must be regarded as not belonging to any of the romantic groups, but as a work of the same order as *Le Rouge et le Noir* and *Madame Bovary*'. And there was tragedy beneath Pushkin's 'serenity' and 'perfect balance'. 'For all its lucidity', *Evgenii Onegin* rose out of a desperate conflict inherent in the social structure of the times and reflected in Pushkin's own tragic life, a conflict dramatized in the opposition of 'the natural humanity of Tatyana (the heroine) to the social values of Evgenii' that 'set a theme which was to be developed through the whole of Russian art and thought.' 'Lenin, like Tolstoy,' Wilson concluded, 'could only have been possible in a world where this contrast was acutely felt.'

Just as apposite to modern times, and especially to Russia, was the theme of another of Pushkin's great poems, 'The Bronze Horseman', which Wilson defined as 'the tragic contradiction between the right to peace and happiness of the ordinary man and the right to constructive domination of the state'. He made his own translation of it, and this translation, 'into prose with an iambic base', so as 'to avoid the woolliness which is the bane of translations of Pushkin – who is the least woolly of poets', is the best of all English versions. It succeeds, as rhymed attempts do not, in rendering the poem's fearful passion, 'embodied in a language of density and energy which are hardly to be found in English outside the first books of *Paradise Lost.*'

These were Wilson's first comments on Pushkin. Afterwards, at different times, he spoke of other works. He pointed out how in *The Gavriliada*, an early mischievous poem that, in the eighteenth-century manner of Parny, travesties the legend of the Immaculate Conception, Pushkin excelled his source through his 'faculty for making anything he touched humanly sympathetic' and his capacity for achieving a perfect correspondence between sound and sense. He detected in *The Gypsies* an intimation, done in 'a series of touches and never too explicitly', that its hero, Aleko, was guilty of a crime from which he was fleeing and that he would 'inevitably commit another' – an example of Pushkin's subtlety and psychological insight. And, having found a discussion that fascinated him of Pushkin's so-called 'Petersburg Tales' in *Articles on Russian Poetry*, a little-known book of 1922 by Vladislav Khodase-vich, he took up the author's analysis of the tales and carried it further by suggesting how Pushkin may have dramatized in them – they are all late works and all permeated by a sense of uncanny evil – the unhappy condition in which he found himself.

One of his essays, a general appreciation of Pushkin, is a gem of literary criticism. I know of nothing else that equals it for compre-hensiveness, economy and grace. It is as if, through force of imagina-tive sympathy, Wilson has become so perfectly identified with his subject, that he reproduces in his own work the qualities he is des-cribing. 'The emotion that we get from reading Pushkin', he writes, 'is something outside the picture; it is an emotion, half-comic, half-poignant, at contemplating the nature of things. . . . We always feel . . . in reading Pushkin, that there is something behind and beyond, something we can only guess at; and this makes his peculiar fascination – a fascination which has something in common with the inexhaustible interest of Shakespeare, who seems to be giving us his sonnets and *Hamlet* and *Lear* and the rest as the moods and dreams of some drama the actuality of which we never touch.'

In 1965, when Vladimir Nabokov published his translation of *Evgenii Onegin*, Wilson's criticism of it provoked a long, ferocious and witty debate. In *A Window on Russia* Wilson reprinted his original piece, with a few emendations, and added a brief, somewhat acerb, but astute estimate of Nabokov's achievement as a novelist.

And once he made a note contrasting a melancholy lyric which Pushkin had written just three years before the fatal duel into which he was goaded, when he sensed 'the forces of Evil . . . closing in' on him, with Alfred de Musset's 'J'ai perdu ma force et ma vie', written 'when he was only thirty and had still seventeen years before him'. 'What is striking about these two pieces is that Musset at thirty feels that he has lost everything, even his belief in his genius, and that the only good thing now left him is sometimes to have wept. . . . Pushkin, although rather wistfully, on the eve of extinction, is still full of creative vitality and planning to find leisure for productions that, one assumes, like those of the past, will express something more than his sorrows.' One cannot read this without a pang of admiration and of grief, for it was written in 1970, when Wilson's health was failing and he had but two more years to live, two years in which, as always, and like Pushkin, he would 'express something more than his sorrows'.

V

If gathered together, Wilson's comments on Pushkin would form a fairly comprehensive essay, but his only sustained piece of criticism on a Russian writer comparable to those on Housman, Flaubert or Henry James is the essay on Turgenev, 'Turgenev and the Life-Giving Drop', which he wrote as an introduction to David

Magarshack's translation of Turgenev's *Literary Reminiscences and Autobiographical Fragments*. This is an exquisitely sympathetic and perceptive study of Turgenev's character and life in relation to his writings. His work, steeped in 'an atmosphere of unrelieved sadness', as Henry James described it, Wilson saw not as the kind of maundering self-indulgence that he was always denouncing, but as the effect of an overwhelming experience of tragedy, to have transmuted which into works of beauty was an act of heroism and a manifest triumph. Turgenev's stories, he wrote, 'show the permanent stamp of an oppressive, a completely hopeless and permanently harrowing experience', the experience of inhuman brutality in the household where he was brought up, and of which his mother was the evil genius. A rich landowner, whose native cruelty was not restrained by any law, she dominated her serfs and her children with the capricious tyranny of absolute power. Her dominance was crushing, it all but paralysed Turgenev's will. But he came out of it, as the little boy in the story from which the title of the essay is taken escaped from the cave of monsters, and was saved by 'the life-giving drop', the precious gift of art. It is to this biographical aspect that Wilson gave his attention, in part, of course, because it was appropriate to the writings which his essay was intended to introduce but also because, as in his essays on Housman, Flaubert, Dickens and others, he wished to deal with such angles of an artist's life and work as were not usually considered, for he had always aimed, he said, 'either to present some writer who was not well enough known or, in the case of a familiar writer, to call attention to some neglected aspect of his work or his career'.

Of Chekhov he sought to correct the usual impression that he was a melancholy purveyor of a misty 'twilight atmosphere'. In an appreciative review of two books on Chekhov, Ronald Hingley's and David Magarshack's, and in the preface to his own selection of some of his late stories, *Peasants and Other Stories*, he emphasized Chekhov's humor and the 'compact and dense' quality of his work, 'all made up of hard detail and larded with allusions to specific things'; and, having straightened out the chronological sequence of his stories, presented those in his own collection as constituting 'a kind of analysis of Russian society, a miniature Comédie Humaine'.

'I hope', he concluded, 'that this volume may help redeem Chekhov, one of the tersest, most lucid and purposive of writers, from the Anglo-Saxon charges of vagueness, to give something of his true weight and point for readers who may have been bewildered by reading him in scrambled collections.' Of Gogol he wrote that with 'the stifling and stagnant' life he depicts, 'there is always something else that creates suspense – an element of the passionate, the *détraqué*'. He perceived 'the typical situation in Gogol' to be 'the sudden falling out of the bottom of some impressive construction that we have watched being elaborately built' and, in a superb description of his style, said that his pages resembled 'the tangled forests and the overgrown gardens that are a recurrent motif' in his work.

About Tolstoy he was ambivalent; on the one hand, he was repelled by his arrogance, vanity and self-centeredness – from the note in his diary when he was twenty-five, 'Once for all I must accustom myself to the idea that I am an exceptional being', to the magisterial tactlessness with which he treated his family and friends, his 'conversion' and asceticism and his supposedly egalitarian attitude to the peasantry, all of which appeared to Wilson to be hypocrisy and exhibitionism; and on the other hand, he was impressed by the greatness of his writing, when it was not, as in his later stories, *The Death of Ivan Ilych, Father Sergius, Master and Man*, 'deformed by the moralistic bias'. He remembered, as late as 1971, the exhilaration of his first reading *War and Peace* in the original. It was after his trip to the Soviet Union:

> I was then living alone in the country in Connecticut beside the small Mianus River. I was buried in a fairly large forest with not another house in sight. I would begin to read and write after dinner and not go to bed till four in the morning. It was winter, and the only drive was covered with snow. I could imagine myself perfectly in the country house of the Bolkonskys. . . .
>
> I was surprised to find the book so amusing. . . . The atmosphere was anything but bleak. And the vitality of the characters was amazing. Tolstoy is perhaps – in a less

caricatured way from those of either Dickens or Proust – the greatest mimic in fiction, and this is something that cannot be brought over in translation.

Although he 'did not always know which syllable of a Russian word should be stressed and could not have read a page aloud correctly, the voices of the characters,' he wrote, 'in my winter solitude, seemed to come right out of the pages and to animate my little house'; and in his own spirited English version, he reproduced, with infectious delight, examples of these living voices.

One of Wilson's finest essays is the first one he wrote on *Doctor Zhivago*, 'Doctor Life and His Guardian Angel', an extraordinary feat of interpretation, in which, within the space of a book review, he disentangles the skein of its highly complicated plot and reveals the intricacy and elaborateness of its closely woven pattern. He shows how 'one finds, threaded in and out of the story, a phase-by-phase chronicle of Soviet policy . . . a discussion of the development of Russian literature', and also 'an historical–political fable . . . of the kind that since the time of Turgenev, has been traditional in Russian fiction'. It is 'one of the very great books of our time . . . a great act of faith in art and in the human spirit'. It will 'come to stand', he predicted, 'as one of the great events in man's literary and moral history', and the children of Pasternak's 'enemies in his fatherland . . . over their vodka and tea, will be talking about the relations between Larisa Fyodorovna and Pasha and Yury Andreye-vich, as their parents, and I don't doubt they themselves, have talked about Tatyana and Lensky and Evgenii Onegin, Natasha and Prince André and Pierre.' Wilson admired the book's symbolic power, the grand sweep of its universal vision in which historical events, 'the Bolshevik seizure of power, the Civil Wars, the Soviet state after Lenin's death, the purges, and the war against Germany', all touched upon in a way that was 'heartbreakingly explicit', appeared, nevertheless, 'as striking local occurrences . . . as the transient phenomena they are', so that for all its reality and precision, 'in spite of its immediacy of detail', Pasternak's work was not a historical novel, nor indeed a novel at all, but 'a legend, a fable' that exhibited 'something of the technique and the spirit of the *skazka*, the Russian folk tale'. It was focused not at all on life in twentieth-century Russia but on the great theme of death and resurrection. So impressed was Wilson by this symbolism that several months later he published a second article, 'Legend and Symbol in Doctor Zhivago', in which, with the help of two friends who were making a close study of the book from this point of view, he presented more detailed evidence of its symbolic aspect, and, in my opinion, carried his investigation to absurd lengths, for once, belaboring a good idea too hard. But his essential view that 'the whole book is an enormous metaphor for the author's vision of life' is scarcely arguable.

VI

As the years passed, Wilson became increasingly disillusioned with the Soviet Union, in which his hopes for man's salvation were further than ever from being realized. He was disaffected with the Russian people who were not living up to his expectations of them, and he now saw them as agents, rather than victims, of the age-long tyranny they were perpetuating. He liked Russians very much, he said, in *A Piece of My Mind*, but found something 'alien' in them, 'something deeply antipathetic' in their native predisposition to hopelessness and lethargy that was embodied in their language and manifested in their art. He had moments when 'after a prolonged immersion, say, in Musorgsky's music or in one of the nineteenth-century novelists', he felt, as even such a sympathetic observer as Melchior de Vogüé had felt before him, 'a kind of disgust and revulsion,' and longed to be refreshed 'with the bell-clear melodies of Mozart or even with Wagner's heroics'. And their maddening language, with so much beauty and so much power, and at the same time so little precision, so carelessly wild and nonchalantly riotous, reflected the supineness, negligence, submissiveness and inefficiency that always irritated Wilson in his dealings with Russians and that now, as he thought about the deterioration of their government and their art, brought out the Ivan the Terrible in him more than ever.

Long before, Wilson derided in the work of the poet Tyutchev an

'incurable minor key of resignation to grievance and complaint',
even though his language was 'delicious and exquisite' and he was
'the great Russian master of the pregnant and pointed and poignant
short poem'. But Tyutchev was 'a little too weepy for our taste',
his tone was 'associated with a humidity of emotional atmosphere'
that made 'the English-speaking reader, in his exploration of
Russian literature . . . instinctively withdraw his hand' as if he had
'come upon something clammy'. And his irritation mounting, as
further clammy illustrations came to mind in the work of other
Russian writers, even of Chekhov and Dostoevsky, though in
modified form, Wilson ended by denouncing all these Russians,
'masticating and gulping and regurgitating their problems, biting
upon their suffering and doting over their guilt, sweating and freez-
ing for years in the *impasses* of personal involvements as if they were
waiting in Soviet breadlines or the reception rooms of callous
officials'.

And now, in one of the last things he wrote, an essay on
Solzhenitsyn, having congratulated 'the Nobel Prize judges on
honoring this very courageous man and very gifted writer,' he
admitted that while he admired his work as 'the most thorough-
going exposé of Stalin's insane tyranny', he was, as 'an Anglo-
Saxon reader', depressed and outraged by 'these chronicles of
senseless suffering, of protracted degradation and torment'. In the
end the Anglo-Saxon becomes 'impatient with beings who are
thus oppressed. Such a state of things', he feels, 'should not be
allowed to exist. Such relations between human beings are certainly
quite abnormal. The existence of a Stalin, after all, implies the
existence of a nation that will stand for the horrors he inflicts.'
And, with a stubborn unwillingness to recognize the lonely
spiritual triumphs of Solzhenitsyn's tragic heroes, he decided that
there was something masochistic in Solzhenitsyn, that 'sheer
endurance' was 'his only theme'.

In 1952 Wilson indulged himself in 'A Modest Self-Tribute', in
which he said that he prided himself on having 'tried to contribute
a little to the general cross-fertilization of cultures' by bringing
'into one system . . . the literatures of several cultures which have
not always been in close communication'. He wished 'as a practicing

critic, to break down the conventional forms . . . that always tend to keep literature provincial'. He attained this purpose, and nowhere more splendidly than in his Russian studies, as lovers of Russian literature the world over are bound to acknowledge, recognizing, even though they may on occasion disagree with some of his judgements, that his self-tribute is all too modest. And with gratitude and admiration, they are bound to honour his remarkable achievement; and can do no less. They can do no less than honour his achievement and express, as best they can, some small measure of their infinite gratitude and admiration.

DAVID FLUSSER

✤

Not Obliged to Any Religion

In his important book about the Dead Sea Scrolls the late Edmund
Wilson devoted one of the best chapters to a talk with me. There he
has written about me that I am 'not obliged to any religion'. A
German scholar, in the ensuing 'Battle of the Scrolls' interpreted
those words, saying about me that the religion of my fathers
became foreign to me. In fact, though originating from an assimilated family, I had become an observing Jew. Wilson's passage
about my position toward the religion was first published in the
New Yorker and my friends asked me to write to Wilson in order
to correct his statement. At the beginning I declined to do so. I
recognized that my person in Wilson's book was not autonomous;
it had a clear function in Wilson's arguments. And would not it be
strange if Hamlet should protest against Shakespeare's distortions
or Dr. Faustus against his description by Marlowe or Goethe?
Finally, under the pressure of my friends, I reacted and sent a
letter to the *New Yorker*. After some months, the letter was returned
to me with the note: 'Not at Hotel New Yorker' and I was glad
about it. So the thought overwhelmed the poor reality.

I like very much Wilson's approach to the questions of religions
and ideologies and his personal understanding of religious phenomena. He, in reality was a man 'not obliged to any religion', and
at the same time a man with a genuine understanding of the various
trends in the religious life of humanity. I had the impression that
he understood religion and ideology as a special kind of contact
between reality and both human spirit and intellect. I think that I
was not wrong, when, by an instinctive reaction, I drank with
Edmund Wilson to the Holy Spirit.

The Holy Spirit is a peculiar kind of progressive element; but, as it has to work in men, it cannot work fully and directly. It runs through ways and tunnels which do not fit its very nature. Partially, the spirit by its impetus can change the complex ways, in order to approach to its aim, but it is bound by human nature and the existence of human society. Thus, in order to progress, the spirit develops religious thought and ideologies, and there is no question that this adaptation of the spirit to the concrete circumstances is very often dangerous. The story of the necessary errors of the Holy Spirit and its partial victories is fascinating. Edmund Wilson was a passionate spectator of this eternal drama and was amused by it. No wonder that the Essene experiment rightly evoked Wilson's interest. Essenism as phenomenon is an outstanding example of the *grandeurs et misères* of the Holy Ghost.

The study of ancient Judaism is an uneasy enterprise. To understand it, you need a lot of knowledge and intuition. I can witness that Wilson knew far more than can be seen from his beautiful book. I have never seen any scholar who could, as Wilson did, understand without difficulties a fluent translation of Hebrew texts into ancient Greek. And he knew sufficient Hebrew in order to read these texts in their original Hebrew. But not only special knowledge in particular fields is needed when you study the Dead Sea Scrolls. Without an interest in various fields of human spiritual history, you cannot understand the very nature of the Essene experiment. You have to make comparisons even with such movements and religious ideologies which have historically nothing to do with the Essenes. Only because of his large and deep erudition was Edmund Wilson able to pave the way for a better understanding of Essenism. From the second edition of his book we see, for instance, how he succeeded in describing the very nature of Mormonism. It was Wilson's intellectual vivacity which enabled him to write his book. Wilson's greatest merit is that he was the first author who discovered Essenism as a peculiar religious phenomenon, as a specific and unique movement.

In his character, in his vast erudition and in his curiosity, Edmund Wilson was in reality a man of the eighteenth century. His humanistic approach to the problem fits the period of enlightenment. This could be a critique if Wilson were a simplistic rationalist as many figures of the eighteenth century enlightenment were. But Wilson was not so; he appreciated all the sides of the spiritual adventures of mankind and his attitude toward the irrational sides of religious experience was positive. Almost nothing human was foreign to him. He resembles in this point the German poet and philosopher G. E. Lessing. Incidentally it was Lessing who caused, as Wilson did, also a kind of 'Battle of Scrolls', and even the object of the battle was the same, namely the meaning of Christianity. Lessing published fragments of a violent German anti-Christian deist, and Wilson has written a book about the Dead Sea Scrolls and clearly formulated the importance of these texts for a new evaluation of Christianity. Even the opponents of these two men were practically the same: conservative Christian theologians were in both cases stricken by fear, thinking that a dangerous assault against their religion had taken place. Once Lessing's greatest opponent, Herr Hauptpastor Goeze, remarked scornfully: how can a writer of comedies write about theology? Lessing replied that a writer of comedies is indeed able to write about theology, but that a theologian is unfit to write comedies. Lessing was not only a dramatic author, but also, among other things, a philosopher and an important author of essays about aesthetics and literature. This enabled him to inaugurate a new era of modern study of Christianity and especially of the New Testament.

Goeze's remark against Lessing expressed the opposition of specialists against independent thinkers. The reaction of so-called specialists in connection with Wilson's book about the Dead Sea Scrolls was similar. Thus, we have to say some words about what is today understood under specialists and 'popularization': these two items are today interconnected. Something happened evidently in our century, especially on the continent of Europe, and this development influenced also other countries. In the past, when Mommsen wrote his *Römische Geschichte*, nobody saw in his monumental work a popularization, even if the book is comprehensive. The same Mommsen has also written special studies, but the different kind of writing was not dictated by two separate kinds of approach, but by the object itself. But until recent years, there was a split not only

between the two literary genres of scholarly books, but also a gap
between scholarship and popularization, or in other words journalism. Today, the old harmony seems to be partially re-established by
the simple technical invention, the paperback. But even so, the
main stream of the *Wissenschaft*, whose representatives are articles
in reviews, and monographs which are themselves mostly expanded
articles or a conglomerate of expanded articles, persists. This kind of
product follows almost always its own laws of writing and thinking
and can be read and understood only by a specialist. The decisive
slogan of such authors is 'method', and the logic of this method is
not identical with the laws which were already discovered by
Aristotle. *Petitio principii* and vicious circles are not only not
avoided, but they very often promote in this kind of writing, as
the sages from Laputa said, 'the unspeakable progress of human
knowledge'. The way toward reality, which should be the aim of
scholarship, is often barred by the fact that many scholars build their
own researches upon the unproven theories of their predecessors.
So their works resemble often Babylonian towers, which are
abandoned, when a new kind of 'method' is discovered. Wilson's
book about the Dead Sea Scrolls, written by a 'non-specialist',
filled often the minds of many scholars with rage, because it
revealed, without such intention, the negative qualities of the so-
called method and 'systematic thinking' and writing of much
modern scholarship. And Wilson had a quality which is lacking in
the main stream of research about the New Testament and origins
of Christianity: he had an excellent feeling for the ways and
reactions of the human spirit during the long history of mankind.
Because of his experience in various fields and various types of
human groups, he was better predestined to understand the Essene
experiment than many one-sided scholars who think that a specialization in a narrow district is necessary and that an extensive erudition
is incompatible with true scholarship.

In one point I am prepared to agree with my colleagues. Wilson's
book about the Dead Sea Scrolls would be better if Wilson had
possessed some of the qualities of the so-called specialists, and in
particular their access to precise scholarly knowledge. If you are
occupied with the Dead Sea Scrolls, or with the New Testament,

you can with profit introduce the new texts in the frame of contemporary Judaism and, if you know it sufficiently, by studying a small particularity, you are able to clarify, in a more complete way, the picture of Essenism. A good and deep knowledge of Hebrew and Aramaic deepens the picture and if you can recognize the value even of a single word or phrase in a text, you are fit to pave a new way for important consequences. Wilson was deprived of such a joyous pleasure. What is needed is to possess both the spiritual vivacity of Wilson and the specific erudition of a specialist. But where to find such a man, both sensitive to spiritual phenomena and living in the prison of specialization? But even so, Wilson's book about the Dead Sea Scrolls raised questions which the scholars were forced to answer, and so it changed profoundly the course of research into Essenism and had an important impact upon the study of both ancient Judaism and the beginnings of Christianity. Wilson compelled the scholars to think.

Wilson was, in his own way, 'not obliged to any religion' and this was also a great advantage. Once, Erasmus from Rotterdam thought that true scholarship can be an effective remedy for the crisis of Christian religion, and I think that he was right, but then theologians, who were not true scholars, misused the achievements of Erasmus, But even so, the problem exists if there can be a complete harmony between objective scholarship and the adherence of a scholar to a revealed, 'positive' religion. Can this problem be solved? But today, unfortunately, this real problem is overshadowed by a new situation. The crisis of religious faith has overtaken also the scholars who, when they profess a religion do not clearly know what they really believe or have to believe. On the other hand, they want to write scholarly objective works and articles; they see in the objectivity a virtue. Often, the autonomous 'method' of the majority of modern scholarship makes it possible, even if such scholars do not admit this, that a kind of objective apologetics arises. All who read the polemics of the 'Battle of the Scrolls' can easily recognize what I mean. Thus, the new crisis of religion overshadows the real problem of religion and objectivity.

In such circumstances, Wilson's book about the Dead Sea Scrolls was an important contribution toward a new point of departure of the study of the history of religions. I would think that scholars who treat their own religion which they profess, should do it without any fear; they should try to see their own religion without any inhibition. Only so will they purify their own religion from inhuman trends. This was evidently the opinion of Erasmus from Rotterdam and this opinion is also valid today.

Wilson was not only a man of enlightenment, he was also a humanist. He was not obsessed by the anti-religious rabies of rationalists. He was able to treat sympathetically even such religious and ideological phenomena, which were not his own. He had a deep respect for all the ways and deviations of the Holy Spirit. So he was fit to write his beautiful and important book about the Dead Sea Scrolls. Edmund Wilson, who was not a professional scholar in the field of ancient Judaism and beginnings of Christianity, has written a book, which is from many aspects, a turning-point in the research of the history of religions.

ANDREW HARVEY

❧

Edmund Wilson and Poetry: a Disagreement

What Johnson said of Dryden's work as a critic could well be applied to Edmund Wilson's: 'Nothing is cold or languid: the whole is airy, animated, and vigorous: what is little is gay: what is gay is splendid'. The strengths of Wilson's criticism of poetry are the strengths of his criticism in general; a passionate and subtle sense of the connections between Literature and Life: a reverence for reality: a refusal to be tempted away from the work of art into dogma or intellectual gamesmanship: a commitment, above all, to communicate delight and a precise awe. There are few more delicate accounts of the creative development of a poet than Wilson's essay on Yeats in *Axel's Castle:* his charting of the influence of Laforgue on Eliot is a model of its kind – precise but not pedantic, concerned to illuminate Eliot's mastery not parade his own erudition or perceptiveness: Wilson's analysis of the incongruity between Valéry's effect as a poet and his theory of poetry is an exhilarating and crafty piece of necessary sabotage; when Wilson writes, of 'Cimetière Marin', that 'in attempting to clear up Valéry's meaning, one clears up too much . . . the proper response is to follow the natural evolution of the poem . . . in that is its challenge and beauty', he shows himself possessed of a rare and accurate critical humility.

Nevertheless, Edmund Wilson's criticism of poetry does have distinct limitations. Chief among these, perhaps, is a limitation of scope. He never engaged with much of the world's greatest poetry – that of the Greek, Elizabethan, and French Classical theatres. He never wrote at any length on Goethe or Dante, Pope or Chaucer, Baudelaire or Horace – our loss, since he had the languages to do so, and the range (how luminously he might have written on the Horace Odes, if he'd chosen to). He wrote no book-length study of any major poet, and did not plan to, as far as I know. You cannot imagine Wilson, like Johnson, writing happily and at length about elision and caesura and whether or not a long poem should be written in rhyme or blank verse – he was not particularly fascinated by poetic technique, as his own poems, with their conventional rhythms and largely unadventurous forms, illustrate. Wilson always quotes well – which is, as Eliot remarked, the surest sign of critical acumen – but unlike Eliot he rarely expands or glosses his quotations; they are there to decorate a critical argument. There is nothing in Wilson's work to compare for technical and philosophical concentration with Leavis's close-readings of Hardy, for instance, or his marvellous discussion of the *Four Quartets* at the end of *The Living Principle*; Wilson does not seem to have engaged with poetry at that intent, quarrelsome depth. His criticism lacks the true poet's inwardness and concern with how the *use* of language reveals and composes meaning – that intensity that illuminates Eliot's driest *dicta* and redeems Arnold's earnestness from the pomposity that is constantly threatening it, that sudden radiance of insight or celebration that makes reading Johnson's *Lives of the Poets* so thrilling an experience. By comparison with such models, even the best of Wilson's essays on poets – the Yeats, for example – seem rather tame and unattached. It is only very occasionally in his criticism of poetry that Wilson makes his own ideas and concerns felt; where he is most authoritative is in his essays on Flaubert, Proust and Joyce; evidently the Novel could engage the whole of his mind as Poetry could not.

Not only does Wilson lack range as a critic of poetry, he can also lack insight and sympathy. He was, for instance, capable of writing: 'Wallace Stevens has a fascinating gift of words that is not far from a gift of nonsense rather like that of Edith Sitwell.' The two are very dissimilar as writers, in aim and achievement; the diction of 'Harmonium' is far more adventurous and controlled than anything in Edith Sitwell; what Wilson is registering is his bewilderment by, and insensitivity to, a certain type of non-referential poetic discourse. What would he make of St. John Perse or Celan, for example? His defence of Edna St. Vincent Millay cannot be described as other than gallant – whatever its formal and sentimental virtues, her work cannot possibly sustain the claims of major status he made for it. In a late interview, Wilson praises Elizabeth Bishop for how 'she ripples out her poems like fluid diaphanous scarves'. Nothing could be less evocative of her style and approach, of 'Man-Moth 'of 'Fish' than 'diaphanous scarves'; Bishop is clear and transparent, certainly, but very tough-minded. Thinking of the Cantos, Wilson wrote: 'You have had the verse technique of Pound turning gradually into a prose technique' – while, in fact, Pound in the Cantos was aiming for (and often achieving) a more subtle and musical *poetic* technique, as a glance at Pound's own critical writings should have shown him. To call the *Four Quartets*, as Wilson did, 'a long muttering with a few flames of vivid speech', is to show oneself insensitive to the rhetorical demands of a long meditative poem, as well as patronizing. Of course, no critic is free from prejudice or misconstruction; Wilson's, however, are revealingly casual; they do not seem marked by any definite critical personality, 'the momentary impatience or blindness of a continual passion'.

There are places, too, where Wilson's great gift for succinct generalization betrays him into pomposity and crudity. How helpful is this remark: 'Thus the theorems of the physicist were matched by the geometrical plays of Racine and the balanced couplets of Pope'? What exactly does 'matched' mean there? Exactly in what ways are the theorems and the couplets linked? When Wilson writes that Rimbaud's *Une Saison en enfer* shows 'the nineteenth-century hysteria of France . . . as crystallized in the sharp and dazzling fragments of what Verlaine called a "diamond" prose' isn't he both generalizing too crudely and taking over a rather silly remark by Verlaine? In what sense is it valuable to think of *Une Saison en enfer* as prose? Is 'diamond' any more than an impotent gesture towards an adjective? Can the work be both hysterical *and* diamond? Isn't the attempt to place so amazing and original a work in such a way rather demeaning as well as vague? After all, if it's only 'nineteenth-century hysteria' that the work is 'representing' (albeit in a 'diamond prose'), why should we bother to read it?

Wilson's delight in historical 'analysis' has more dangerous effects than crudity – it leads him, I think, to depreciate the range and potential of modern poetry. In his essay on Yeats he writes: 'It was easy for the lyric poet, from Wyatt's age to Waller's, to express himself both directly and elegantly, because he was a courtier, or, in any case, a member of a comparatively small educated class, whose speech combined the candour and naturalness of conversation among equals with the grace of a courtly society. It was possible for him honestly to take up a residence in an intellectual world where poetic images stood for actualities because the scientific language and technique for dealing with these actualities had not yet come to permeate thought. But', he adds, 'the modern poet who would follow this tradition, and who would yet deal with life in any large way, *must* [my italics] create for himself a special personality, *must* [my italics again] maintain a state of mind which shall shut out or remain indifferent to many aspects of the contemporary world.' It is possible to agree with much of the analysis but disagree completely with the conclusion – why 'must' the poet create for himself 'a special personality'? Is this what Neruda or Brecht or Montale, in their very different modes, have done? What aspects of the 'contemporary world' has Auden closed himself off from? To describe Yeats as 'indifferent to many aspects of the contemporary world' would surely be to underestimate the reach and implication of his work – enraged yes, or appalled, but not 'indifferent'! In the second half of this essay I want to deal more specifically with this myopia or defeatism in Wilson's thought.

★　　★　　★　　★

The title of Edmund Wilson's essay 'Is verse a dying technique?' suggests the answer which is found in the essay itself; 'As time goes on and the technique of prose tends to take over more and more of the material which had formerly provided the subjects of verse, and as the two techniques began to appear side by side or combined in a single work . . . surely it is time to discard the word "poetry" or to define it in some other way, so as to recognize that the most intense,

the most profound, the most comprehensive, and the most beautifully composed works of literary art . . . have been written sometimes in prose and sometimes in verse, depending chiefly on which
literary technique happens to be dominant at the period.' Of course,
the dominant literary technique of our time is clearly prose. In this
Wilson is in excellent company. In his analysis of the rise of the
Novel Hegel had shown how thoroughly the Novel had usurped the
function of Heroic Poetry, how attuned prose was as a medium to
our 'prosaic sense of reality' and to the nineteenth century and the
bourgeois class which dominated and moulded it: Tocqueville had
argued, following Hegel, that prose was the democratic medium
par excellence, and likely not merely to take over the central
social role of Heroic Poetry but to make all poetry obsolete,
except some simplistic forms, such as the folksong or music hall
ballad, which are immediately absorbable by a people too brutalized
by work, too levelled by competitiveness, too imaginatively and
spiritually deprived by an increasingly godless and technocratic
society to want or be able to appreciate anything more complex or
more exalted. Among English writers, Pater is Hegel's most
elegant and aesthetically prescient heir. As he puts it in his essay on
'Style': 'Prose not verse is the special and opportune art' of the
modern world: what characterized the nineteenth century for him
was 'a restless condition of mind little susceptible to the restraint
proper to verse form . . . and secondly, an all-pervading naturalism,
a curiosity about everything whatever as it really is, involving a
certain humility of attitude cognate to what must after all be the
less ambitious form of literature'. For Pater, this expansion of the
role and range of prose was extremely exciting – 'And prose thus
asserting itself as the special and privileged artistic faculty of the
present day will be, however its critics may narrow its scope, as
varied in its excellence as humanity itself reflecting on the facts of
its latest experience – an instrument of many stops, meditative,
observant, descriptive, eloquent, analytic, plaintive, fervid. Its
beauties will not be exclusively pedestrian; it will exert in due
measure all the varied charms of poetry, down to the rhythm
which, as in Cicero or Michelet, or Newman, at their best, gives its
musical value to every syllable.'

Wilson seems excited about how exact this prophecy was: 'Prose is showing itself', he writes, 'quite equal to the work of the imagination and the intellect.' And who reading *Ulysses*, *A la Recherche du temps perdu*, *The Death of Vergil*, *To the Lighthouse*, *Light in August* could disagree – each of them written in a complex intense prose inconceivable except as a possiblity to prophetic critics like Pater before the turn of the century, each of them works of the highest imaginative range and vitality? In her essay 'The Narrow Bridge of Art', Virginia Woolf dreams of a prose that can express 'the discord . . . incongruity . . . curiosity . . . [of modern life] . . . the quick queer emotions that are bred in small separate rooms . . . the wide, general ideas which civilization teaches', that 'would have some of the exultation of poetry . . . be dramatic, and yet not a play', that would be 'so humble it can go anywhere . . . no place . . . too low . . . too sordid . . . too mean for it to enter'. And indeed this dream of an omnivorous and omnipotent and omnicompetent prose no longer seems a challenging fantasy but an actuality. With the decline of verse drama, and the unlikelihood of its successful revival, it is in prose, it seems, that the major imaginative works of our time are being written, and in a prose, too, that is almost infinitely expressive and self-renewing.

Where does this leave Poetry, however? Must it cede its ancient dignity and scope completely to the New Prose? Has Poetry, then, no special function, no particular claims to make on the devoted concentration of both reader and writer? Has Tocqueville's chilling vision of a society ignorant of the true glories and complexities of Poetry and incapable of appreciating them now been realized? It is in what I think are his implicit 'replies' to such questions that Edmund Wilson is most pessimistic and disappointing. Half-way through his essay he gives some of his prejudices away: 'The trouble is that no verse technique is more obsolete today than blank verse. The old iambic pentameters have no longer any relation whatever to the tempo and language of our lives.'

The first sentence is plain wrong and the second based on an unsubtle and unhelpful notion of what the relationship between a poet (or any other kind of writer) and his time and society is, or, worse, should be. After all, Yeats and Stevens, arguably the two greatest poets in English of the century, both wrote continually in the pentameter, finding it and making it completely adequate to the complexity of their visions. What is it that fails 'the tempo and anguage of our lives', for instance, in the last stanza of 'Among School Children'? –

> Labour is blossoming or dancing where
> The body is not bruised to pleasure soul,
> Nor beauty born out of its own despair,
> Nor blear-eyed wisdom out of midnight oil.
> O chestnut-tree, great-rooted blossomer,
> Are you the leaf, the blossom or the bole?
> O body swayed to music, O brightening glance,
> How can we know the dancer from the dance?

If there is anything that fails to correspond here, we'd better reconsider the 'tempo and language of our lives'. The question is not so much of correspondence as of response – response to that crisis of tempo, order and language that is today universally felt. Stevens addresses this even more explicitly than Yeats, in the last lines of 'The Idea of Order at Key West':

> Oh! Blessed rage for order, pale Ramon,
> The maker's rage to order words of the sea,
> Words of the fragrant portals, dimly-starred,
> And of ourselves and of our origins,
> In ghostlier demarcations, keener sounds.

So neither for Yeats nor for Stevens was the use of the pentameter archaic or unnatural – they used it with complete ease and individuality. When Pound tried to make Eliot expunge from the Game of Chess in *The Waste Land* the line 'filled the desert with inviolable voice' because it was 'too penty' not only was he attacking a moving and beautiful line, but he was also expressing a local historical prejudice which Eliot was sensible enough to ignore on that occasion – if not sensible enough not to repeat on others. As Pater reminds us in his essay on 'Style', 'Critical efforts to limit art *a priori* are always liable to be discredited by the facts of artistic production.' Pound and Wilson should have known better. The pentameter and the forms it has traditionally filled are still alive. To claim otherwise is to ignore or perhaps even devalue the practice of many of our most exciting contemporary poets – poets who have not abandoned the attempt to establish a fruitful and responsible correspondence of the present with the past and its traditions of rhythm and form. And this leads to misplaced despair and a kind of melodramatic ignorance.

However, it isn't just the Great Recent Dead who were able to use the pentameter and the forms it filled to masterly and passionate effect. Larkin's 'Church Going', for instance, could almost be seen as an inventory of what the pentameter and form can achieve in skilled contemporary hands. From the hesitant invocation of a distinctly modern mood in –

> Once I am sure there's nothing going on
> I step inside, letting the door thud shut.
> Another church; matting, seats, and stone,
> And little books; sprawlings of flowers, cut
> For Sunday, brownish now . . .

to the satirical meditations in which this mood is questioned –

> I wonder who
> Will be the last, the very last, to seek
> This place for what it was; one of the crew
> That tap and jot and know what rood-lofts were?
> Some ruin-bibber, randy for antique,
> Or Christmas-addict, counting on a whiff
> Of gowns-and-bands and organ pipes and myrrh? . . .

Through to the rich bleak music of the end where in a high diction – and lyrical openness of rhythm, past and present join –

> A serious house on serious earth it is
> In whose blent air all our compulsions meet,
> Are recognized, and robed as destinies.
> And that much never can be obsolete,

> Since someone will forever be surprising
> A hunger in himself to be more serious
> And gravitating with it to this ground
> Which, he once heard, was proper to grow wise in,
> If only that so many dead lie around.

Through all these shifts of focus and tone, Larkin manages to make of the pentameter a perfectly supple and natural medium for expressing his deepest (and very contemporary) thoughts about society and religion. Like his great masters Yeats and Hardy, Larkin has succeeded in marrying simple and unaffected speech to intricate form; it is because of this success that the sombre 'old-fashioned' sonorities of the last stanza do not strike the reader in any way as willed or imposed – Larkin's feat is to make them emerge naturally and with an unobtrusive, unemphatic urgency from their setting. They have been earned, and in earning them for the poem, the poet has also earnt them for us – their 'tempo and language' have been made our own.

Critics less responsible than Wilson but in agreement with him when he writes that 'the trouble is that no verse technique is more obsolete today than blank verse,' have also alleged that the special barbarity, inhumanity, and horror of contemporary society have made all traditional modes and forms of expression absurd. Might not exactly the opposite be the case? Might it not be true that we can only face the absolute terrors of our time by the displacement, formal control, responsible and sober lucidity of address, that traditional modes of expression make possible? Take, for instance, another poem by Larkin – the 'Old Fools':

> What do they think has happened, the old fools,
> To make them like this? Do they somehow suppose
> It's more grown-up when your mouth hangs open and drools
> And you keep on pissing yourself. . . .

What might have been shapeless – the poet's agonized pity for the horror of ageing – is contained here by the form into which it has been cast – contained not in the sense of being muted, or tamed, or given a furtive and unearned dignity, but of being chastened into sobriety and clear height. The poet moves us more by this control, helps us to understand and share more responsibly his sense of outrage than he would if he had given it undisciplined vent; by this control he also shows us that the outrage and pity which he feels we must share need not destroy or unman us, because it has not destroyed or unmanned him, that we have means of understanding and clarity that will be equal to the challenges, however devastating, of life. To teach us that sense of courageously unillusioned adequacy to what History and Life might have in store for us is, I think, one of the contemporary poet's chief tasks, and more achievable, perhaps, within the radiant discipline of traditional form than outside it.

But Larkin is perhaps too 'obvious' and 'traditional' an example even if his stature makes it difficult to ignore him. Lowell may be more promising for the 'democratic correspondence' that Wilson seems to want for his poets. In *Notebook*, for instance, he wanted (and found) a medium 'a rough blank verse' in which he could mould all his current preoccupations. Without the control of blank verse, the limitations and verbal spruceness enforced by it and the unrhymed sonnet form in which he wrote *Notebook* that work would have been even more sprawling, and far more self-indulgent, than it is. Precisely because he was risking an extreme and varied confessionalism, Lowell felt he needed the discipline of form to prevent that openness from becoming loose or embarrassing. Like Larkin, in fact, Lowell is a master at manipulating the pentameter in a thoroughly contemporary way. Take, for instance, 'Harriet' – the first sonnet from *Notebook* –

> Half a year, then a year and a half, then
> ten and a half – the pathos of a child's fractions, turning
>   up each summer. God a seaslug, God a queen
> with forty servants, God . . . she gave up – things whirl
> in the chainsaw bite of whatever squares
> the universe by name and number. For
> the hundredth time, I slice through fog, and round
> the village with my headlights on the ground,
> as if I were the first philosopher,

as if I were trying to pick up a car
key . . . it can't be here, and so it must be there
behind the next crook in the road or growth
of fog – there blinded by our feeble beams,
a face, clock-white, still friendly to the earth.

Here Lowell rubs the rhythms of his own thoughts against the traditional suggested rhythms of the pentameter; by eluding the perfect iambic until the last line he beautifully mirrors in the music of the poem the hesitations of which it is talking – the relief of seeing 'a face, clock-white, still friendly to the earth' is embodied in the calm rhythm of the regular pentameter after so many fragmented ones.

Geoffrey Hill is a harsher, bleaker, and less social poet than either Larkin or Lowell, and his use of the pentameter and traditional form is even less seductive or ably manipulative. His masterpiece *Funeral Music* – one of the few works of our time to confront its brutality without sentimentality or hysteria – is written in a fiercely high diction and rhythm which one would have thought impossible for a contemporary poet to bring off until Hill did. He makes us believe, as only a formidable artist can, that the strange tortured language he uses is the only one possible for his vision. Like Larkin and Lowell, but in a more ironic way, Hill uses the pentameter, its traditional rhythms and expectations, to his own ends. The last sonnet of *Funeral Music* illustrates this well –

Not as we are but as we must appear
Contractual ghosts of pity; not as we
Desire life but as they would have us live,
Set apart in timeless colloquy:
So it is required; so we bear witness
Despite ourselves, to what is beyond us,
Each distant sphere of harmony forever
Poised, unanswerable. If it is without
Consequence when we vaunt and suffer, or
If it is not, all echoes are the same
In such eternity. Then tell me, love,
How that should comfort us – or anyone

Dragged half-unnerved out of this worldly place,
Crying to the end 'I have not finished'.

A bleaker statement of the human condition it would be difficult to imagine. We are 'contractual ghosts of pity'; if we bear witness to 'what is beyond us' it is 'despite ourselves'; our suffering might well be useless, and we die 'crying to the end "I have not finished"'. Nevertheless, as Santayana said of Macbeth's speech 'Tomorrow and tomorrow and tomorrow' – 'the very fact that he can speak with such eloquence about absurdity is itself the most eloquent of qualifications of that absurdity'. Hill has won a dignity, a bitter, clear passion, from his apprehension of isolation and perpetual frustration – that dignity and passion are inseparable from the form metre and that has earned them. For Hill has had the courage 'to go on wrestling with the mighty dead . . . and to make of this ghostly struggle a fresh sublimity' (Bloom). No relationship with the traditions of the past, at this late and highly self-conscious stage of our culture can be without anxiety and stress; what is certain, however, is that strong poetry will only emerge from an attempt to forge and sustain that relationship, with whatever ambivalence, and at whatever risk. If creative health were still possible, it might be of the kind Goethe envisaged when talking to Müller about Byron in 1824 – 'He is much too patient with people who accuse him of plagiarism – merely skirmishing in his defence instead of bringing up heavy artillery and blowing his opponents sky-high. Do not all the achievements of a poet's predecessors and contemporaries rightfully belong to him? Why should he shrink from picking flowers where he finds them? Only by making the riches of others our own do we bring anything great into being.' Perhaps it is, now, impossible to imagine any relationship with the past so exuberant and unselfconscious (Goethe himself pitied the English for having so great a literature to emulate), but I think the relationship Goethe envisaged should be the model for all modern poets. As Socrates said of his Just City: 'Whether such an one exists, or will ever exist in fact, is no matter; for he will live after the manner of that city, having nothing to do with any other' (Book 9 – *The Republic* – Jowett's translation).

What, then, of that second sentence of Wilson's 'The old iambic pentameters have no longer any relation whatever to the tempo and language of our lives'? It is obviously inadequate to – even if it were desirable in – the practice of some of our best contemporary poets. What is more, it is based on an inadequate and misleading view of the nature and role of poetry as a whole.

Is a poet's justest response to the jumble and chaos of his time to write in a correspondingly jumbled and chaotic way? Is it incumbent on him as a kind of moral duty, to write about his time, or from his time, in its own terms, to be fragmented where it is fragmented, hysterical where it is hysterical? Might not poetry be valuable precisely because of the private attentiveness it demands, because it is language not necessarily 'to the tempo' and 'in the language' of our lives but at the fullest power and most exact intensity the poet can attain? Wordsworth wrote in his Preface to the *Lyrical Ballads*: 'Aristotle, I have been told, hath said that poetry the most philosophic of all writing; it is so; its object is truth, not individual and local, but general and operative; not standing upon external testimony, but carried alive into the heart by passion.' How a poet grasps and manifests that truth will always be mysterious but surely it has never been and will never be by any simple-minded relation to 'the tempo and language of our lives' – nor should we judge it by that criterion. Is any great poetry of the past great *because* it mirrored 'the tempo and language' of the lives of its society? How could Hölderlin or Hopkins, intense solitaries both with an extremely private and wrought language, be praised for that? Is *Paradise Lost* great *because* it reverberates with the drums and rhetoric of the Civil War? Style, as Pater reminds us, is the man 'not in his unreasoned and really uncharacteristic caprices, involuntary or affected, but in absolutely sincere apprehension of what is most real to him'. What was most real to Yeats, for example, what he apprehended with absolute sincerity, has very little to do with 'the tempo and language of our lives' – he saw that tempo and that language as being fundamentally destructive of the life he worked to celebrate and preserve. In the last section of his 'Meditations in time of Civil War' he writes –

127

The cloud-pale unicorns, the eyes of aquamarine,
The quivering half-closed eyelids, the rags of cloud or of lace,
On eyes that rage has brightened, arms it has made lean,
Give place to an indifferent multitude, give place
To brazen hawks. Nor self-delighting reverie,
Nor hate of what's to come, nor pity for what's gone,
Nothing but grip of claw, and the eye's complacency,
The innumerable clanging wings that have put out the moon.

It is against that 'grip of claw', that 'eye's complacency', and in
scorn of the 'innumerable clanging wings that have put out the
moon' that Yeats wrote as he did. Are we not the richer for that
rebellion against what he thought of as the cheapness of his time,
that scorn of its 'tempo and language'?

Is prose really so completely expressive a medium as he claims?
Few writers can have exulted as comprehensively in the achievement
and possibilities of prose as Virginia Woolf. Yet, as she tells us, the
novelist risks 'poetic intensity' at peril to the coherence of his
work – 'the trouble with the purple patch being not that it is
purple but that it is a patch'; 'A prose writer may dream dreams and
see visions, but they cannot be allowed to lie scattered, single,
solitary upon the page . . . for prose has neither the intensity nor the
self-sufficiency of poetry. It rises slowly off the ground; it must be
connected this side and that. There must be some medium in which
its ardours and ecstasies can float without incongruity, from which
they receive support and impetus.' In her essay The Narrow Bridge
of Art she continues, 'can prose, we may ask, adequate though it is to
deal with the common and the complex – can prose say the simple
things which are so tremendous . . . can it leap with one spring at
the heart of its subject as the poet does? I think not. That is the
penalty it pays for having dispensed with the incantation and the
mystery, in rhyme and metre.' The very range of prose is also its
limitation; 'You cannot cross the Narrow Bridge of Art carrying
all its tools in your hands. Some you must leave behind, or you will
drop them in mid-stream or, what is worse, overbalance and be
drowned yourself.'

In so hysterical and materialistic a time as ours poetry is important

precisely because of the height of its address, precisely because of its refusal to be beglamoured by the values, and 'tempo and language' of a time that threatens its life. It may look to the past not the present for its food and support – and if that gaze is passionate enough, clear enough, unillusioned enough it may be of immense importance to the present, accusing it and mocking it into an uncharacteristic dignity and calm – Beauty, as Hopkins puts it, will have been kept back 'from vanishing away'. In a time, too, when the 'language of our lives' has become so debased, so corrupt with cliché and jargon, words without any colour, or charm, or gladness, Poetry is valuable precisely because of its inveterate concern to use language at its most radiant. As Pound reminds us Literature's function has to do with the clarity and vigour of 'any and every thought and opinion':
. . . 'when this work goes rotten – by this I do not mean when they express indecorous thoughts – but when the very medium, the very essence of their work, the application of word to thing goes rotten . . . the whole machinery of social and individual thought and order goes to pot'. In a time too, when human creativity in all its forms, all things 'counter, original, spare' are threatened, to limit poetry to the 'tempo and language of our lives' is to hold it from its unique power of preserving our inmost lives from destruction. As Shelley says, 'Poetry defeats the curse which binds us to be subjected to the accident of surrounding impression. And whether it spread its own figured curtain, or withdraws life's dark veil from before the scene of things, it equally creates for us a being within our being. It makes us the inhabitants of a world to which the familiar world is a chaos . . . and it purges from our inward sight the film of familiarity which obscures from us the wonder of our being. It compels us to feel that we perceive and to imagine that which we know. It creates anew the universe, after it has been annihilated by the recurrence of impressions and blunted by reiteration.' To create 'a being within our being', to 'purge from our inward sight the film of familiarity' to restore us to 'the wonder of our being' that is poetry's true task, and one impossible to fulfil if it is too slavishly and unimaginatively yoked to the 'tempo and language of our lives'.

That Wilson can be so defeatist about the future of poetry is not entirely surprising, given the generally meagre quality and ambition of contemporary verse. It is shaming to read Wordsworth's description of the poet as the 'Rock of defence of human nature . . . an upholder and preserver carrying everywhere with him relationship and love' and then read most of what is now published as poetry. Not that this is of course entirely or even mainly the poet's fault – historical factors outside his control have limited his audience and therefore his range. Nevertheless, as Virginia Woolf wrote to John Lehmann, the self of much modern poetry is 'a self that sits alone in the room at night with the blinds drawn'. The poet is much less interested in what we might have in common than in what he has apart. That this need not be the case she was certain, 'why should not poetry now that it has so honestly scraped itself free from certain falsities, the wreckage of the Great Victorian Age, now that it has so sincerely gone down into the mind of the poet and verified its outlines . . . why should it not once more open its eyes, look out of the window, and write about other people . . . you have it within you to deal with a vast variety of subjects; it is only a temporary example that has shut you up in your room alone with yourself'. What then is needed from a critic who is concerned with the future of a great literary art is not prematurely to mourn its passing but to examine what is happening and try, however hesitantly, and with whatever reservations and sense of uncertainty, to point to ways in which it might regain its old dignity. As Virginia Woolf wrote 'There are a thousand voices prophesying despair. Science, they say, has made poetry impossible – there is no poetry in the motorcar and wireless. And we have no religion. All is tumultuous and transitional. Therefore, so people say, there can be no relations between the poet and the present age. But surely that is nonsense. These accidents are superficial; they do not go nearly deep enough to destroy the most profound and primitive of instincts . . . the instinct of rhythm . . . what I mean is, summon all your vigilance, exert all your courage, invoke all the gifts that Nature has been induced to bestow.'

JOHN WAIN

The Daughters of Earth and the Sons of Heaven: Edmund Wilson and the Word

During the threnodial period after Edmund Wilson's death, it appears to have been conventional to refer to him as the last American man of letters. One hopes this was no more than an expression of that facile pessimism always so attractive to the literary temperament. So much of the spirit of a nation is caught and stabilized in its literature, and not only the classic literature of the past but the current output, that the man of letters (he who to a greater or lesser degree knows about it and evaluates it, and to a greater or lesser degree contributes to it) is a figure that no society can do without. As well try to get along without the philosopher, the jurist, the historian.

While in no way eager, then, to share the doom-and-gloom outlook that makes Wilson 'the last' American man of letters, one starts any assessment from the knowledge that an American man of letters is very firmly what he was. His work, in both creative and critical *genres*, arises always, and derives much of its energy always, from his twin sense of what he could usefully do in literature and what he could usefully do in America. He lived into a demotic era that insists on measuring everything by the standards of a mass society, so that in age he struck people as lonely and aristocratic. But he was never a man of the ivory tower. The need to *serve* the society he lived in – by entertaining and instructing it, by lecturing and scolding and badgering it, even by snubbing it – never left him. In the first conversation I had with him, in 1957, he said, 'I'm sixty-two – I just want to be left alone to write about the past.'

He had indeed just brought out his ample anthology of the American literary tradition, *The Shock of Recognition*, and must have been deep into the even more gigantic task of writing *Patriotic Gore*. But the past he wrote about was the American past, or the European past seen through American eyes, and the lessons he persistently drew from it were lessons for the America he lived in.

One can't love the soul of literature without also loving her body, which is language. Wilson's passion as a man of letters was a fiercely concrete passion, a devouring appetite for everything that made up the literary life. He loved books, he loved print, he loved the atmosphere of libraries*: on that first visit (it was to Talcottville) I took him a parcel of new books from England, and to see him rip the parcel open (like a P.O.W.!) and put the books out on his desk, he with so many decades of reading behind him, was to glimpse something of the passion that must have driven a Johnson, a Hazlitt, a Sainte-Beuve. (After we had talked fairly late and I went to bed, he stayed up reading the books hour after hour with a bottle at his elbow, and in the morning he was monumentally hung-over.) And he loved language. A book he couldn't read was not, as it is to so many of us, a cemented-up doorway; it was an interesting challenge.

Most of us are very lazy about acquiring languages. We start out

* Cf. his admiring anecdote about Thoreau in *The Shock of Recognition*: 'On one occasion he went to the University Library to procure some books. The librarian refused to lend them. Mr. Thoreau repaired to the President, who stated to him the rules and usages, which permitted the loan of books to resident graduates, to clergymen who were alumni, and to some others resident within a circle of ten miles' radius from the College. Mr. Thoreau explained to the President that the railroad had destroyed the old scale of distances – that the library was useless, yes, and President and College useless, on the terms of his rules – that the one benefit he owed to the College was its library, – that, at this moment, not only his want of books was imperative but he wanted a large number of books, and assured him that he, Thoreau, and not the librarian was the proper custodian of these. In short, the President found the petitioner so formidable, and the rules getting to look so ridiculous that he ended by giving him a privilege which in his hands proved unlimited thereafter.'

in our twenties with the rudiments of two or three of them, driven somehow into our heads at school and college; we add a smattering of another one or two, as the accidents of our roving youth take us here and there; but, usually in our thirties, we settle down with our limitations, what we have we have, and we begin to read more and more in translation; at first shamefacedly, but increasingly with the belief, as life presses in on us with duties and responsibilities, that even to read in translation is a worthy enough aim. Not for Wilson.

Starting at the Hill school with a fair grip on the classics ('Greek was then far more attractive to me than Latin'), and on the more familiar Western European languages, he added Russian and then Hebrew in middle life; and in age, Hungarian. For the Russian he had the incentive of travel and of his interest in social experiment; for the Hebrew there were also sound utilitarian reasons; but the Hungarian study seems to have been dictated by pure literary enthusiasm; he had heard that there was an interesting literature there, and he had a distaste for breathing the stale air of translation; though, as he engagingly said, 'I must say that I set out on this exploit with a slightly uneasy memory of the senile Baron Hulot in Balzac tottering up to the attic to begin his last liaison.'

To you and me, learning a new language is an exhausting chore, or would be if we ever did it. To Wilson it was evidently a fascinating game. He liked puzzles (cf. his fondness for card games and his joy in composing witty light verse with 'amphisbaenic' rhymes and all the rest of it), and a new language enlivened him with fresh puzzles to solve. In the delightful essay 'My Fifty Years with Dictionaries and Grammars' (*The Bit Between My Teeth*, 1966) he has described for us the element of play and recreation in his linguistic studies.

A foreign language commits you to nothing: by amusing the mind, at first, with technical problems of grammar and the accents of a new vocabulary, it frees one from one's pressing immediate problems and from the tone of one's own community. . . . And in the meantime one is getting new insights – always, I find, surprising – into the way in which other people live, or have lived, in other parts of the world, and the infinite variety of ways in which they conceive their existence.

Obviously this is all great fun; but working at a language, whichever way we look at it, is *work*, and Wilson's readiness to take trouble is an important ingredient in his character. And not his personal character only. It is an ingredient in the historical role he saw himself as playing, one imposed on him as much by his ancestry, and by the moment of his appearance onstage, as by his personal choice.

'Everyone knows' Wilson's own account of his two main objectives, as he set them out in 'Thoughts on Being Bibliographed' (1943). In his youth he had admired Shaw and Mencken ('prophets of new eras in their national cultures . . . carrying on that work of "Enlightenment" of which the flame had been so fanned by Voltaire'), but soon realized that there was no point in fighting those battles over again. There remained two areas of interest—modern developments in the theory and practice of literature, and the impact of Marxism on the international scene. (The passage is quoted in full by Mr. Sharratt on p.61.)

It will be noticed that this statement of Wilson's aims is made almost entirely in social terms; on the face of it, neither task – the bringing of modern literature to the attention of the American bourgeoisie, and the imparting of glad tidings about social experimentation in Russia – would seem to call for much verbal sensitiveness, much attention to precise and specific literary effects. But Wilson's practice was always stoutly independent of his theory. (cf. his wonderfully take-it-or-leave-it employment of Freud's category of the 'anal erotic' in the essay on Ben Jonson: the three main characteristics of the type are '(a) orderliness . . . in an over-accentuated form, pedantry; (b) parsimony, which may become avarice; (c) obstinacy, which may become defiance and perhaps also include irascibility and vindictiveness'. Wilson refuses to become involved with Freud's theories, and is thoroughly sceptical of the view that the workings of the alimentary tract have any cause-and-effect relationship with the personality; but he is 'sure that Freud has here really seized upon a nexus of human traits that

are involved with one another and has isolated a recognizable type',
to which Jonson belonged.) He understood that criticism is a
pragmatic discipline, pressing towards generalization perhaps, but
always through the analysis of particular effects. His work is
always concrete: he reacts to what is in front of him. In *Axel's
Castle* he makes a conscientious – and entirely sincere – plea for an
approach to art quite different from that of the European Symbolist
writers he has been studying; and he blows a resounding fanfare
now and then, affirming democracy and social consciousness: the
most celebrated being his peroration to the chapter on Proust,
quoted by Mr. Sharratt on p.63.

But the strength of *Axel's Castle* does not come from its socially
laudable intentions: it comes from the passion, and clarity, and
fierce responsive concentration, with which Wilson reads what is on
the page. And these qualities are rooted, as they must be, in a
veneration for language as the storehouse of information and
emotion, the most subtle and particularizing form of human
communication.

In late middle age Wilson was given to an amusing and mock-
ferocious lambasting of slovenly modern linguistic usage. *Deceptively
simple, by any standards, breakthrough, love–hate relationship, mitigate
against, naked force* – in rapid succession they fell to his fowling-
piece. (I notice, by the way, that *reportage* earns his disapproval –
'why not simply reporting?' Since I shall use the word in this essay
to describe a part of Wilson's own work, I feel impelled to pipe an
uneasy defence: French journalism has traditionally featured the
series of commissioned articles on a topical subject, contributed not
by a staff writer but by an outside person who might not be a
journalist at all, might indeed be a man of letters like Wilson himself,
and, while this kind of ultra-respectable journalism is not confined
to France, it has given *reportage* a resonance that *reporting* doesn't
quite have.)

Essays like 'Current Clichés and Solecisms' are the fruit of
Wilson's later sixties; but many years earlier, right from the start,
he had shown a watchful awareness that such as the language was,
the literature would be. He was generous in attributing some of
this awareness to his teachers, notably Christian Gauss ('He made

us all want to write something in which every word, every cadence, every detail, should perform a definite function in producing an intense effect'), but clearly it was native to him. Part of the fascination exercised over the young Wilson by Edna St. Vincent Millay (he was in love both with the woman and her work) came from her 'thrilling' way of reading her poetry. Looking back in 1952, he recalled that 'she pronounced every syllable distinctly; she gave every sound its value', and mused, 'I believe that our failure in the United States to produce much first-rate lyric poetry is partly due to our flattening and drawling of the vowels and our slovenly slurring of the consonants; and Edna spoke with perfect purity.'

Many critics, on both sides of the Atlantic, would of course dispute that judgement hotly, though it seems to me that Wilson had a point; it is not first-rate poetry that is relatively scarce in American literature, but first-rate *lyric* poetry, and certainly in the most widely admired American poetry of the last seventy years one hears the speaking voice far more often than the singing voice. And Wilson makes an exception of E. E. Cummings, who whatever his deficiencies was undeniably a lyric poet: 'Cummings has, like Edna, the New England precision in enunciating every syllable. All three [he is speaking of Millay, James Joyce, Cummings] are masters of tempo and tone.' Over ten years later, he was praising Robert Lowell by saying, 'he is, I think, the only recent American poet – if you don't count Eliot – who writes successfully in the language and cadence and rhyme of the surrounding English tradition'.

Wilson's rootedness in language, his appetite for varied verbal fare, sent him often to the poets. But this is not the time or place to conceal the fact that his taste in poetry was not, in fact, much better than average. His acceptance of conventional reputations is one pointer to the limitations of his verbal and rhythmic sensitivity: so is his uncomprehending hostility to the idea of keeping alive minority languages when majority ones are available: 'why cultivate tongues that are dying out or that will only be learned by the people of a relatively small nationality at the expense of those of wider currency?' (*A Piece of My Mind*, p. 55). His studies of poets have the same good qualities as his studies of prose writers; he relates them to the world, as when in *Axel's Castle* he convincingly defends Yeats against the charge of being an airy-fairy trifler. Yet that same essay on Yeats contains an example of his rather blunt-fingered approach to poetry, when he drags a few lines out of context and fails to notice just what the context was. Describing Yeats's work in 'the period inaugurated by *The Green Helmet*', Wilson says,

> When he returns to the heroic world of Irish mythology, he describes it with a new homeliness of detail. And more and more steadily he fixes his attention upon the actual world about him. He has come to desire above everything, as he says in another part of the poem about the fisherman:

> > To write for my own race
> > And the reality.

Now the lines that Wilson slightly misquotes here come, of course, from 'The Fisherman', a poem that occurs in *The Wild Swans at Coole*, the next volume but one after *The Green Helmet*, and form part of a meditation on Ireland. The fisherman, in his grey Connemara clothes, who climbs at dawn to a mountain pool to fish for trout, embodies one kind of Irishness; the brawling, pushing urban mob, the new middle class who were in fact seizing the reins of power in Ireland, whom Yeats disliked and was disliked by, represent the antithetical kind. He is announcing a choice, that he identifies with, and writes for, 'this wise and simple man' beside his trout-pool, but he knows the price that is to be paid and he knows that this choice stems from disappointment and disillusion – he has tried to work with, and write for, the politicking, fixing, newspaper-reading urbanites and the experience has been a bitter one.

> All day I'd looked in the face
> What I had hoped 'twould be
> To write for my own race
> And the reality;
> The living men that I hate,
> The dead man that I loved,

The craven man in his seat,
The insolent unreproved,
And no knave brought to book
Who has won a drunken cheer,
The witty man and his joke
Aimed at the commonest ear,
The clever man who cries
The catch-cries of the clown,
The beating down of the wise
And great Art beaten down.

Wilson, intent on making his (perfectly valid) point about Yeats's greater involvement with human life as opposed to faery, snatches two lines out of context and quotes them in a meaning that they do not bear in the poem. I do not mean that none of us who write criticism ever misquote or get things wrong; but I do mean that a man who relished Yeats's poetry word by word and line by line, as it ought to be relished, would not have made that particular mistake.

Still on the subject of Wilson's approach to poetry, an interesting example of it, showing both the faults and virtues, occurs in chapter 12 of *Patriotic Gore*, which discusses the poetry of the Civil War. Obviously the best poet who made any serious attempt to write about the war was Whitman, and Wilson recognizes this and quotes some good poems; but the poet who catches his attention most is the half-forgotten Southern writer Sidney Lanier. First we get a sketch of Lanier's life and circumstances, written with a warmth and sympathy that engages our interest in Lanier as a man and a brother. Then comes a general assessment of his literary achievement which certainly does not err on the side of praise ('Though sensitive, Lanier is limited, sometimes a little stupid') but, once again, leaves us with a warm and admiring sense of a man who did the best that was in him and made genuine sacrifices for his art. Wilson quotes a passage from one of Lanier's letters that, if we knew nothing else about him, would be enough to give us a respect for the man; he sees him as a mouthpiece, whether conscious or instinctive it hardly matters, of the sorrow and bitterness of the defeated South: he 'projects' into emblematic situations 'the self-annihilating fury of his people'. ('His people'; the pronoun expresses Wilson's deeply-rooted belief that the poet does not stand apart from his age and generation, he stands among them and utters their moods and aspirations.) And then Wilson quotes the whole of 'The Revenge of Hamish', a narrative poem in a strange experimental metre. This metre, Wilson tells us off-handedly, is 'logaœdic dactyls', that is, 'an informal kind of classical metre, which permits a loose handling of metrics and is an example of the technical experimentation which appears in Lanier's later poems'.

I do not know whether the information about logaœdic dactyls is to be found in Lanier himself or whether Wilson recognized the form as such. In either event it is characteristic of him to note that the form is unusual, to indicate briefly what the poet found in it, and to call it by its right name. (Mingling dactyls and trochees, or anapaests and iambs, it achieves a blend of verse-rhythms and prose-rhythms, of λόγος, speech, and ἀοιδή, song.) The poem is indeed very interesting rhythmically: here are the first two stanzas:

It was three slim does and a ten-tined buck in the bracken lay;
And all of a sudden the sinister smell of a man,
Awaft on a wind-shift, wavered and ran
Down the hill-side and sifted along through the bracken and
                                        passed that way.

Then Nan got a-tremble at nostril; she was the daintiest doe;
In the print of her velvet flank on the velvet fern
She reared, and rounded her ears in turn.
Then the buck leapt up, and his head as high as a king's to a
                                        crown did go
Full high in the breeze . . .

The story of 'The Revenge of Hamish' is simple and stark. A Scottish highland laird, wishing to cut a fine figure in the sight of his wife and young son, has resolved to kill a red deer as a spectacle for them. To this end the deer must be driven towards him and not allowed to leap the burn and make their escape. Hamish, tall and strong but growing old, is set this task; he fails, and the deer escape;

the laird savagely orders him ten lashes (for the ten tines of the stag's antlers) laid on hard enough to draw blood at each stroke. He submits, while the retainers stand round silent and ashamed; the laird then withdraws, leaving wife and child unguarded; Hamish suddenly snatches the child and runs up to a precipice above the sea. He will drop the boy to his death unless the laird in his turn receives ten lashes. After a struggle with his pride, the laird yields to his wife's passionate entreaties and is flogged. The mother goes up to Hamish to take her child back, drawing eagerly closer:

> Till her finger nigh felt of the bairnie's face –
> In a flash fierce Hamish turned round and lifted the
> child in the air,
> And sprang with the child in his arms from the
> horrible height in the sea,
> Still screeching 'Revenge!' in the wind-rush.

There are a number of comments one might make on this poem even without going beyond the ground Wilson has chosen, the historical and social. It tells us important things about the literary culture from which it comes: the fact that a Southern American poet dramatizes the plight of his people in a story set in the Scottish Highlands probably indicates the continuing influence of Scott throughout the English-speaking world, and thus, through one important channel, of European Romanticism; while the bookish, classically-derived form of the poem emphasizes that Lanier's roots are in a literate society. But the most striking feature of the poem, obviously, is the violence and narrowness of the passions it describes. Scott himself, as a good Edinburgh bourgeois, was fascinated by the Highland character with its blood-feuds, its quasi-Sicilian code of personal honor, its determination to kill or die rather than abate its pride. All these features exist in the Southern temperament; they were disapprovingly caricatured by Mark Twain in *Huckleberry Finn*, and have been described countless times. It is this that Wilson seizes on:

> The arrogant attitude of Hamish, leaping with the child in his arms, is a parable of the action of the South in recklessly

destroying the Union. . . . Tall Hamish the henchman dies
poisoned – by hatred, by the lust for revenge. Sidney Lanier in
this piece is a dramatic poet, and that spirit has spoken through
him.

The last sentence, there, is not quite clear to me: is it the spirit of
dramatic poetry, or the spirit of hatred and reckless vengeance,
that has spoken through Lanier? If the latter, I should feel happier
with a little more attention to ethical and emotional *nuance*. Does
Lanier – does the poem, that is – feel admiration at Hamish's
reckless acceptance of death, or horror at his murder of the innocent
child? Both, I think; and it is here that Hamish's action is most fully
emblematic of the desperate Southern resistance and subsequent
ruin, because an essential part of Southern society was the black
slave population, who were treated exactly as children are treated
in every society – cruelly by cruel people, kindly by kind ones,
but in any case never as equals. By leaping off the cliff with the
child in his arms, Hamish is involving the helpless and unconsulted
in his ruin. The poem embodies not only the blind vengefulness of
the dying South, but its streak of insane callousness also.

As the Lanier example serves to remind us, there was no essential
difference between Wilson's approach to poetry and his approach
to prose. By treating Lanier's poem as 'a parable', he has put it in
the same domain as a work of prose fiction. This approach had its
limitations, but in the literary context of Wilson's epoch it was, I
think, an advantage. That epoch saw such a proliferation of arcane
theorizing about poetry that it must have been for many readers a
relief to find a critic of Wilson's authority who saw no need of such
theories, who walked straight up to a poem and talked about it as
if it were a Tellurian object and not one that had just landed from
another planet. The 'New Criticism' of the 'forties was in itself a
useful movement, reacting away from mass standards, concentrating
on deep verbal analysis and the attainment of value–judgements
through exhaustive attention to the particular; but, in retrospect,
even the best of its practitioners look fussy and limited beside
Wilson's scope and freedom. (Which has lasted better, Wilson or
R. P. Blackmur?) Eliot spoke of 'the preposterous suggestion that

criticism can be an autotelic activity'; in the twenty years that followed, many writers, including some who were self-proclaimed disciples of Eliot, acted as if that suggestion were true; in such an age, Wilson stood out as a rock of sanity, as he continues to stand out amid the excesses of Structuralism and psycho-criticism. He went straight for the things that concerned him, and what concerned him were the basic issues of life, and conduct, and the quality of a civilization.

In this respect his literary criticism is much better than his social and political writing – better, that is, on the same ground. He analyses a social pattern far more sensitively when he has it encapsulated in a work of literature than when it is diffused into generalities. (His social *reportage* is another matter; it has the concreteness and impact of his literary criticism, being substantially the same thing – a response to what is in front of him.) 'An Appeal to Progressives', for instance, a piece that Wilson published in the *New Republic* during the first onset of the Depression and reprinted in *The Shores of Light*, starts off briskly with a terse and concrete description of the breakdown of laissez-faire capitalism, the discontent of the people, the running-dry of the traditional American virtues and the failure of any new ones to materialize in their place; but in the latter part of the essay, where Wilson is suggesting what should be done – in the 'appeal' itself – a tide of cliché and platitude comes dismayingly pouring in: don't be afraid of the Russian example, take politics out of the hands of the politicians, etc., etc. Of course it is always harder to say what should be done than to point to what is wrong, but still it is possible to think constructively and to think about real things, and Wilson towards the end of this essay is simply coining slogans. How different, in its memorability and compassion and strong flavour of reality, is a piece like 'Hull House in 1932' (to be found in *The American Earthquake*)!

In the event, America recovered from the Depression – largely thanks to that European War of which Wilson disapproved, and which he thought America should stay out of – and the diseases of American life altered their nature; razzamatazz instead of dejection, overconfident materialism instead of breadline poverty, the burdens of a 'world role' instead of the limitations of provinciality.

Wilson broadened his fire, but he never ceased to preach, to say to his society, 'Thou ailest here, and here'. In the Preface to *Patriotic Gore*, in *The Cold War and the Income Tax*, he thundered against American expansionism, against the hypocrisy that announces noble war aims and avoids owning up to competitiveness and greed. Setting aside the question of whether the United States is actually guilty of these things, or more so than any other nation – since nations notoriously behave collectively much worse than they do as individuals – that was his target.

Edmund Wilson's view of American society – of any human society, perhaps – was ultimately a tragic one. While some of the more glaringly obvious outrages might be put right, social reform could go no further without running into insoluble problems. In America the conflict between North and South, between industrial and pre-industrial, had ended by stamping out the Southern way of life, which included getting rid of the degrading institution of slavery; but, after all, the forces that had triumphed were not much better.

The Northerner is sure to be shocked when the Southerner speaks frankly of the Negroes as creatures – an inferior race – for whom political or social equality is utterly and forever unthinkable. But the position of the Northerner himself depends upon human exploitation. He may, of course, be entirely unaware of it, not know who makes the clothes he wears, prepares the food he eats, digs the fuel that heats him or pours the steel for the building he lives in – he may not even know where the money comes from that enables him to buy all those things; but though his consciousness may be more innocent, he is none the better off for that. And the Southerner, on his side, becomes suspicious of the Northerner's pretensions – smelling hypocrisy in his humane anxieties, mania in his moral idealism, and in his eternal insistence on 'service' an attempt to make up for, to palliate, the savageries of a mechanized society self-seeking and rapacious in the highest degree.

So he wrote in an essay of the nineteen-thirties, 'Tennessee Agrarians'. Already the optimism of youth was behind him and he was perceiving life as the usual sad human muddle, in which anything recognizable as 'progress' turns out to be the displacement of one set of habits by another – the new habits being free of the more obvious disadvantages of the old, but importing new disadvantages of their own.

This being the pattern of his thinking, it was inevitable that sooner or later his purview of American history should come to include the lonely figure of the Red Indian. The nudge that actually started his active interest in Amerindian history appears to be described in the opening paragraph of *Apologies to the Iroquois* (1960):

> In the summer of 1957, a young English writer came to visit me in the little town in upstate New York in which I have since childhood spent many of my summers. As we were driving back one day from the county fair, I retailed to him, with an air of authority, a scrap of information which I had only lately acquired: that the name Adirondack meant, 'They eat bark', and had been applied by certain Indians to other Indians that lived in the mountains which were visible, as we drove, in the distance. My visitor asked me what had become of the Indians, and I replied that there were only a few of them left, scattered in reservations. He inquired about the Mohicans, and I told him they were the same as the Mohawks.

It so happens that I was the (then) 'young English writer' who asked the casual question and jogged into motion the powerful machinery in the skull of the short pear-shaped man sitting beside me. I realize, of course, that such credit as I can claim from the incident is trivial, since Wilson would have arrived at the Iroquois sooner or later simply by following the trajectory of his own thoughts; still, I take a modest pride in the involvement. He had already (1947) written a study of the Zuñi Indians of California, but their strange and remote society he viewed from outside; his chief interest was in their spectacular ceremony, the Shálako, and he approached it in the spirit of an anthropologist. The Iroquois, by contrast, were part of the America that he saw as his own natural habitat; their history was intertwined with the history of the grandparents and great-uncles and cousins whom he traced with Yeatsian fascination. And once again, what he found was a rich, tragi-comic confusion of issues, a sombre complication shot through with gleams of joy and courage. (But this part of the story is best left in the hands of Mrs. Crouse Mele.)

As a critic, as a man of letters generally – and, quite simply, as a man – Edmund Wilson was at bottom a historian. The imagination that guided him was the historical imagination. In his relationship with the world, he was aware that countries, institutions, languages, ideas, people, and he himself, were ceaselessly changing and that to comprehend anything is to comprehend the ways in which it is being altered. Hence his relationship with all the major elements in his world – America, Europe, large political ideas, forms of art, the notion of literature itself – was a continuing drama, always unfolding, towards a dénouement that could come only with his own death. Everything he wrote was, in a sense, a progress report; or, as in the case of the brilliant short essay 'A Preface to Persius', a kaleidoscope. He recognized this himself as he got into middle age. The account of his Russian travels (1935) ends with some reflections on the Western European countries and what they had meant to him.

> When one traveled in the early years of the century, the European countries one visited loomed as immense entities, with impregnable national virtues, luminous and civilizing cultures, sacred traditions, majestic histories. At the time of the War, they seemed like Titans colliding. Today when one has been in the United States and then in Soviet Russia, they seem a pack of little quarrelsome states, maintaining artificial barriers and suffering from morbid distempers. How the map seems to have changed since our youth!

This changing relationship was the dynamo of Edmund Wilson's thinking and writing. And we should read him in the same spirit: recognizing that, as regards Europe, *Axel's Castle* still falls within the period when the European countries seemed to him to have 'impregnable national virtues' and 'luminous and civilizing cultures', while *Europe without Baedeker* reflects the period when they seemed little and quarrelsome and a prey to 'morbid distempers'; and that as regards America, his reverence for tradition, his fascinated harking-back to the Kimballs and Reeds and Talcotts, is one side of a coin whose reverse is distaste for the restless commercialism that had come to be dominant in American life. Anyone can fulminate against anything, but Wilson's diatribes against the rubbishy element in American life (a rubbish so eagerly imported into all other countries which were not under a prison discipline) drew authority from the depth of his comprehension of the old rooted America of stone houses and close-knit families and independent ways. American advertising has been a favourite target for satire since it came into being, but a passage like this has the Wilsonian bite because it is backed by the Wilsonian grasp of an older culture.

> Advertising, as we have it in the United States, is a sheer waste of money and brains; but if you allow competitive business for private profit, you have to have a whole corps of poets, artists, preachers, blackmailers and flatterers to compete in selling its wares. It is a formidable undertaking to persuade people to invest at high prices in valueless breakfast foods and toothpastes; in cosmetics that poison the face, lubricants that corrode your car, insecticides that kill your trees; in health-builders made of cheese, fat-reducers containing cascara, coffee made of dried peas, gelatine made of glue, olive oil made of cottonseed, straw hats composed of wood shavings, sterling silver that is lead and cement, woolen blankets, silk stockings and linen sheets all actually woven of cotton, sealskin coats that are really muskrat, mink and sable that are really woodchuck, mahogany furniture of gumwood that will splinter into bits under use; in foods that do not nourish, disinfectants that do not disinfect, shock-absorbers that cause you to ride more roughly and gas-logs for the fireplace that asphyxiate – all articles which have lately been put over with more or less success.

This kind of thing can be reeled off by many a professional anti-American (usually making a fat living out of it, since Americans more than any other people will pay money to hear themselves abused), but Wilson was something else – a social and literary critic deeply committed to his country, not out of chauvinism but out of a wise conviction that if you can't get things right at home you are unlikely to be able to put other people's houses in order.

Let me end on a frankly personal note. Like everyone who reads seriously, I have sometimes turned for help to the critics; not all the time, for the contemporary refusal to read any work of literature without a posse of critics at one's elbow strikes me as simply one more symptom of our cultural dégringolade, and the present-day bookshop with its rows of 'Critical Guide' and 'Critical Heritage' and pre-digested aids generally, fills me with alarm and depression; but often enough, for criticism is a useful art however it may be abused. And, in the course of my reading life, four critics have made more difference than any others to the way I actually read a book. They are: my tutor, C. S. Lewis; Samuel Johnson; William Empson; and Edmund Wilson. Asking myself what these four have in common, I see that they are all both inward-looking – concerned with language, sensitive to the ingredients that go to make a literary effect – and outward-looking; they all value literature as a source of aesthetic pleasure and emotional satisfaction, but even more for its involvement in the world, what it can tell us about ourselves and one another, what it can do for us in helping us to live our own lives.

In all these four critics, I find the same root, language; the same trunk, a strong individual personality; and the same branches, spreading out into wide political and social issues. Edmund Wilson's fascination with language, his 'Fifty Years with Grammars and Dictionaries', is matched by Lewis's book *Studies in Words*; there, on an early page, Lewis remarks,

> I am sometimes told that there are people who want a study of literature wholly free from philology; that is, from the love and knowledge of words. Perhaps no such people exist. If they do, they are either crying for the moon or else

resolving on a lifetime of persistent and carefully guarded delusion.

Yet Lewis's work as a critic was at the furthest possible remove from that of the head-down philologist whose only interest in words is to map their ramifications of meaning. He values philology as the essential tool for comprehending what writers have actually meant to *say*. Similarly with William Empson, famous for his subtle teasing-out of effects in the language of poetry and author of a work of White-Knight lexicography in *The Structure of Complex Words*; no critic has been less afraid of large general issues, soaring up to them from the runways of his patient analyses. Samuel Johnson actually wrote a Dictionary, single-handed; and it was Johnson who said, in words that Edmund Wilson would surely have been glad to echo,

I am not yet so lost in lexicography as to forget that words are the daughters of earth, and that things are the sons of heaven.

THE CRITIC AS ARTIST

CLIVE JAMES

🌿
The Poetry of Edmund Wilson

Apart from *Poets, Farewell!*, which was published in 1929 and has
been unobtainable for most of the time since, the two main collections of Edmund Wilson's verse are *Note-books of Night* and *Night
Thoughts*. Of these, *Note-books of Night* was published in America
in 1942, took three years to cross the Atlantic (Secker & Warburg
brought it out in May 1945) and has since become fairly unobtainable itself, although it is sometimes to be found going cheap in the
kind of second-hand book shop that doesn't know much about the
modern side. *Night Thoughts*, published in America in 1961 and in
Britain a year later, is still the current collection. It regroups most
of the work in *Note-books of Night* into new sections, interspersing
a good deal of extra matter, ranging from lyrics written in youth to
technical feats performed in age. The final effect is to leave you
convinced that, although *Night Thoughts* is good to have, *Note-
Books of Night* remains the definitive collection of Wilson's verse.
Less inclusive, it is more complete.

Being that, it would be an interesting book even if Wilson's
verse were negligible – interesting for the sidelight it threw on the
mind of a great critic. But in fact Wilson's verse is far from negligible. Just because Wilson's critical work is so creative doesn't mean
that his nominally creative work is a waste of time. Even without
Memoirs of Hecate County and *I Thought of Daisy*, the mere existence
of *Note-Books of Night* would be sufficient evidence that Wilson
had original things to say as a writer. It is a deceptively substantial
little book which looks like a slim volume only by accident. There
are more than seventy pages of solid text, with something memorable on nearly every page. Thirty pages are given to prose fragments

and the rest to poetry. It isn't major poetry, but some of it is very good minor poetry – and in an age of bad major poetry there is very little good minor poetry about.

Wilson was no shrinking violet, but he knew his limitations. He knew that his touch with language wasn't particularly suggestive so he went for precision instead. He possessed a lot of information to be precise with. Where his verse is excessive, it is the excess of the seed catalogue – a superfluity of facts. He never usurps the lyrical genius's prerogative of saying more than he knows. Nor did he ever consider himself talented enough to be formless – his formal decorum always reminds us that he stems from the early twentieth-century America which in retrospect seems more confident than Europe itself about transmitting the European tradition. The work is all very schooled, neat, strict and assured. And finally there is his gift for parody, which sometimes led him beyond mere accomplishment and into the realm of inspiration. In 'The Omelet of A. MacLeish', for example, the talent of his verse is reinforced by the genius of his criticism, with results more devastating critically than his essays on the same subject, and more vivid poetically than his usual poems.

In *Note-Books of Night* the poems are arranged in no chronological scheme. From the rearrangement in *Night Thoughts* it is easier to puzzle out when he wrote what, but even then it is sometimes hard to be sure. Eventually there will be scholarly research to settle the matter, but I doubt if much of interest will be revealed touching Wilson's development as a writer of verse. After an early period devoted to plangent lyricism of the kind which can be called sophomoric as long as we remember that he was a Princeton sophomore and an exceptionally able one into the bargain, Wilson quickly entered into his characteristic ways of seeing the world. Like other minor artists he matured early and never really changed. Indeed he was writing verse in the thirties which forecast the mood of the prose he published in the early seventies, at the end of his life. The desolate yearning for the irretrievably lost America which makes *Upstate* so sad a book is already there in *Note-Books of Night*, providing the authentic force behind the somewhat contrived Arnoldian tone of poems like 'A House of the Eighties':

—The ugly stained-glass window on the stair,
Dark-panelled dining-room, the guinea fowl's fierce clack,
The great gray cat that on the oven slept—
My father's study with its books and birds,
His scornful tone, his eighteenth-century words,
His green door sealed with baize
—Today I travel back
To find again that one fixed point he kept
And left me for the day
In which this other world of theirs grows dank, decays,
And founders and goes down.

Wilson's poetry of the thirties frequently deals with houses
going to rack and ruin. The houses are in the same condition that
we find them in forty years later, in *Upstate*. They are in the same
places: Talcottville, Provincetown, Wilson's ancestral lands. Houses
pointing to the solid New England civilization which once found
its space between the sea and the Adirondacks and was already
being overtaken by progress when the poet was young. In his
essays of the thirties (notably 'The Old Stone House' collected in
The American Earthquake) Wilson wrote optimistically about an
America 'forever on the move'. But, if his essays were true to his
then-radical intellect, his poetry was true to his conservative feelings.
His dead houses are metaphors for a disappearing way of life.

And when they found the house was bare
The windows shuttered to the sun
They woke the panthers with a stare
To finish what they had begun.

The poem is called 'Nightmare'. As we know from his great
essay of 1937, 'In Honour of Pushkin' (collected in *The Triple
Thinkers* and rightly called by John Bayley the best short introduction to Pushkin – a decisive tribute, considering that Bayley has
written the best long one) Wilson was particularly struck by the
supreme poetic moment in *Evgenii Onegin* when Lensky is killed in
a duel and his soulless body is compared to an empty house, with
whitewashed windows. The image is one of the climactic points in

all poetry – it is like Hector's address to Andromache, or Eurydice holding out her useless hands, or Paolo kissing Francesca's trembling mouth – so it is no wonder that Wilson should have been impressed by it. But you also can't help feeling that the image was congenial to his personal psychology. Although in books like *Europe Without Baedeker* Wilson did his best to secede from the weight of the European heritage, the fact always remained that by his education – by his magnificent education – and by his temperament he was inextricably committed to an American past which owed much of its civilized force to the European memory. This was the America which was dying all the time as he grew older. One of the several continuous mental struggles in Wilson is between his industrious loyalty to the creative impulse of the new America and his despairing sense – which made itself manifest in his poetry much earlier than in his prose – that chaos could in no wise be staved off. The decaying houses of his last books, with their cherished windows broken and highways built close by, are all presaged in the poetry of his early maturity.

But in some respects maturity came *too* early. Coleridge, perhaps because he had trouble growing up, favoured a slow ripening of the faculties. There was always something unsettling about the precocity of Wilson's mimetic technique; his gift as a parodist was irrepressibly at work even when he wanted it not to be, with the result that his formally precise early lyrics tend towards pastiche – they are throwbacks to the end of the century and beyond. The tinge of Arnold in 'A House of the Eighties' – the pale echo of his melancholy, long withdrawing roar – is compounded even there, it seems to me, by memories of Browning. At other times you can hear Kipling in the background. Wilson's attempts at plangent threnody call up the voices of other men.

Wilson's elegiac lyrics are never less than technically adroit; their high finish reminds us forcibly not only of the standards which were imposed by Christian Gauss's Princeton (standards which we can see otherwise in the poetry of John Peale Bishop) but of a whole generation of American poets, now not much thought about, who had complete command of their expressive means, even if they did not always have that much to express. Edna St. Vincent

Millay and Elinor Wylie have by now retreated into the limbo of the semi-read – Eleanor Farjeon and Ruth Pitter might be two comparable examples from this side of the water – but, when you look at the work of Elinor Wylie, in particular, it is astonishing how accomplished she was. Wilson's criticism helped American writing grow out of its self-satisfaction at mere accomplishment, but he knows about the certain losses as well as the possible gains. In his poetry he committed himself to the past by synthesizing its cherishable tones, but he paid the penalty of mimetic homage in not sounding enough like himself. In 'Disloyal Lines to an Alumnus' he satirized the poetry of Beauty –

> And Beauty, Beauty, oozing everywhere
> Like maple-sap from maples! Dreaming there,
> I have sometimes stepped in Beauty on the street
> And slipped, sustaining bruises blue but sweet . . .

but his own lyric beauty was not different enough from the Beauty he was satirizing. These lines from 'Riverton' take some swallowing now and would have needed excuses even then:

> – O elms! O river! aid me at this turn –
> Their passing makes my late imperative:
> They flicker now who frightfully did burn,
> And I must tell their beauty while I live.
> Changing their grace as water in its flight,
> And gone like water; give me then the art,
> Firm as night-frozen ice found silver-bright,
> That holds the splendor though the days depart.

Give me then the art, indeed. He had the artifice, but the art was mainly that of a pasticheur. When consumed by Yeats's business of articulating sweet sounds together, Wilson was the master of every poetic aspect except originality. Listen to the judiciously balanced vowel-modulations in 'Poured full of thin gold sun':

> But now all this –
> Peace, brightness, the browned page, the crickets in the grass –
> Is but a crust that stretches thin and taut by which I pass
> Above the loud abyss.

A virtuoso is only ever fully serious when he forgets himself. Wilson is in no danger of forgetting himself here. In his later stages, which produced the obsessive technical games collected in *Night Thoughts*, his urge to jump through hoops clearly detached itself from the impulse to register feeling; but it should also be noted that even early on the division existed. His penchant for sound effects, like his ear for imitation, usually led him away from pure expression. On occasions, however, when consciously schooled euphuistic bravura was lavished on a sufficiently concrete subject, Wilson got away from tricksy pastoralism and achieved a personal tone – urbane, sardonic, tongue-in-cheek, astringent. The consonant-packed lines of 'Night in May':

Pineapple-pronged four-poster of a Utica great-great

were a portent of what Wilson was able to do best. Such a line is the harbinger of an entire, superb poem: 'On Editing Scott Fitzgerald's Papers', which first appeared in the preliminary pages of *The Crack-Up* and stands out in *Note-Books of Night* as a full, if regrettably isolated, realization of the qualities Wilson had to offer as a poet.

Speaking personally for a moment, I can only say that it was this poem, along with certain passages in Roy Campbell's bloody-minded satires, which first convinced me that the rhyming couplet of iambic pentameter was still alive as a form – that in certain respects it was *the* form for an extended poem. Wilson, like Campbell, by accepting the couplet's heritage of grandeur was able somehow to overcome its obsolescence: once the inevitable effect of archaic pastiche was accepted, there was room for any amount of modern freedom. In fact it was the fierce rigour of the discipline which made the freedom possible. And Wilson was more magnanimous than Campbell: his grandeur really *was* grandeur, not grandiloquence.

Scott, your last fragments I arrange tonight . . .

The heroic tone is there from the first line. (It is instructive, by the way, that only the tone is heroic: the couplets themselves are not Heroic but Romance – i.e. open rather than closed.) It would have been a noble theme whatever form Wilson had chosen, because Wilson's lifelong paternal guardianship of Fitzgerald's talent is a noble story. Fitzgerald was the Princeton alumnus who *didn't* benefit from the education on offer. From Wilson's and Fitzgerald's letters to Christian Gauss we can easily see who was the star student and who the ineducable enthusiast. But Wilson, like Gauss, knew that Fitzgerald was destined to make his own way according to a different and more creative law. Wilson called *This Side of Paradise* a compendium of malapropisms but knew that it had not failed to live. When the masterpieces arrived he saw them clearly for what they were. Much of his rage against Hollywood was on Fitzgerald's behalf: he could see how the film world's sinister strength was diabolically attuned to Fitzgerald's fatal weakness. He understood and sympathized with Fitzgerald even in his most abject decline and guarded his memory beyond the grave.

Such a story would be thrilling however it was told. But the couplets are ideal for it: the elegiac and narrative strains match perfectly, while the meretricious, Condé Nast glamour of the imagery is entirely appropriate to Fitzgerald's debilitating regard for the high life – the well-heeled goings-on to which, as Wilson well knew, Fitzgerald sacrificed his soul but which he superseded with his talent. Hence Wilson evokes the memory of Fitzgerald's eyes in terms of a *Vogue* advertisement. Passing their image on to what they mint, they

> . . . leave us, to turn over, iris-fired
> Not the great Ritz-sized diamond you desired
> But jewels in a handful, lying loose:
> Flawed amethysts; the moonstone's milky blues;
> Chill blues of pale transparent tourmaline;
> Opals of shifty yellow, chartreuse green,
> Wherein a vein vermilion flees and flickers –
> Tight phials of the spirit's light mixed liquors;
> Some tinsel zircons, common turquoise; but
> Two emeralds, green and lucid, one half-cut
> One cut consummately – both take their place
> In Letters' most expensive Cartier case.

The consummately cut emerald is obviously *The Great Gatsby*; the half-cut emerald is probably *Tender Is The Night*; and we suppose that the tinsel zircons are the hack stories Fitzgerald turned out in order to pay his bills. But apart from the admittedly preponderant biographical element, what strikes you is the assured compression of the technique. In lines like 'Tight phials of the spirit's light mixed liquors' Wilson was forging a clear, vital utterance: that he was to take it no further is a matter for regret. In this poem his complicated games with language are confined within the deceptively simple form and serve the purpose. Here is the public voice which Wilson so admired (and by implication adumbrated for our own time) in the artistry of Pushkin. In 'On Editing Scott Fitzgerald's Papers' his playfulness, his seriousness, his severe humour and his sympathetic *gravitas* are all in balance. The proof of Wilson's mainly fragmentary achievement as a poet is the conspicuous force he attained on the few occasions when his gifts were unified. The artist who is all artist – the artist who, even when he is also a good critic, is nevertheless an artist first of all – can recognize this moment of unity within himself and lives for nothing else but to repeat it. Wilson had too many other interests: which, of course, it would be quixotic to begrudge him.

There are other narrative poems by Wilson but they lack the transforming discipline of the couplet. Similarly he has other strong subjects – especially sex – but as with most revelations their interest has become with time more historical than aesthetic. Yet other poems are full of named things, but the names deafen the vision. Three different kinds of deficiency, all of them interesting.

The first deficiency is mainly one of form. Wilson's narrative poems are an attempt at public verse which certainly comes off better than comparable efforts by more recognized American poets. Nobody now could wade through Vachel Lindsay's *Roan Stallion*, for example. Wilson's 'The Good Neighbour' is the story of Mr. and Mrs. Pritchard, who become obsessed with defending their house against invaders. Wilson guards against portentousness by casting the tale in hudibrastics, but the results, though very readable, are less popular than cute. The technique is too intrusive. Another narrative, 'The Woman, the War Veteran and the Bear', is an outrageous tale of a legless trapeze artist and a girl who married beneath her. It is full of interesting social detail but goes on too long: a glorified burlesque number that should have been a burlesque number. The stanzas are really ballad stanzas, but the poem tries to be more than a ballad. 'Lesbia in Hell' is better, but again the hudibrastics are the wrong form: they hurry you on too fast for thought and leave you feeling that the action has been skimped. Doubly a pity, because the theme of Satan falling in love with Lesbia involves Wilson in one of his most deeply felt subjects – sexual passion.

It still strikes the historically minded reader that *Note-Books of Night* is a remarkably sexy little book for its time. Wilson, we should remember, had a share in pioneering the sexual frankness of our epoch. *Memoirs of Hecate County* was a banned book in Australia when I was young. Wilson lived long enough to deplore pornographic licence but never went back on his liberal determination to speak of things as they were. Poems like 'Home to Town: Two Highballs' convey something of the same clinical realism about sex which made Wilson's prose fiction extraordinary and which still gives it better than documentary importance. In *Memoirs of Hecate County* Wilson drew a lasting distinction between the high society lady, who appealed to the narrator's imagination but left his body cold, and the low-born taxi-dancer who got on his nerves but fulfilled him sexually. The chippie seems to be there again in 'Two Highballs'.

> And all the city love, intense and faint like you –
> The little drooping breasts, the cigarettes,
> The little cunning shadow between the narrow thighs . . .

Paul Dehn, mentioning this passage when the poem was reprinted in *Night Thoughts*, found it ridiculous, but I don't see why we should agree. Wilson's attempts at a bitter urban poetry –

> And the El that accelerates, grates, shrieks, diminishes,
>   swishing, with such pain –
> To talk the city tongue!

are at least as memorable, and certainly as frank about experience, as the contorted flights of Hart Crane. Of Crane, when I search my memory, I remember the seal's wide spindrift gaze towards Paradise and the bottles wearing him in crescents on their bellies. There were things Crane could do that Wilson couldn't – the wine talons, the sublime notion of travelling in a tear – but on the whole Wilson did at least as good a job of reporting the city. And in matters of sex he was more adventurous than anybody – ahead of his time, in fact.

But, if you are ahead of your time only in your subject, then eventually you will fall behind the times, overtaken by the very changes in taste you helped engender. So it is with Wilson's sexual poetry: all the creativity goes into the act of bringing the subject up, with no powers of invention left over for the task of trans-forming it into the permanence of something imagined. Ideally, Wilson's sexual themes should have been a natural part of a larger poetic fiction. But as we see in 'Copper and White' (not present in *Note-Books of Night*, but *Night Thoughts* usefully adds it to the canon) what they tended to blend with was greenery-yallery *fin de siècle* lyricism.

> I knew that passionate mouth in that pale skin
> Would spread with such a moisture, let me in
> To such a bareness of possessive flesh! –
> I knew that fairest skin with city pallor faded,
> With cigarettes and late electric light
> Would shield the fire to lash
> The tired unblushing cheeks to burn as they did –
> That mouth that musing seemed so thin,
> Those cheeks that tired seemed so white!

It is as if Ernest Dowson and Lionel Johnson had been asked to versify Edith Wharton's discovery of passion as revealed in her secret manuscript *Beatrice Palmato*. The very tones of out-of-dateness. But the informing idea – of loneliness in love – is still alive. It should have been the poem's field of exploration, but Wilson was content to arrive at the point where his admired Proust began. Wilson was protective about his selfhood, as major artists never can be.

As to the naming of names – well, he overdid it. Great poetry is always full of things, but finally the complexity of detail is subordinated to a controlling simplicity. Wilson wrote some excellent nature poetry but nature poetry it remains: all the flowers are named but the point is seldom reached when it ceases to matter so much what kind of flowers they are. In 'At Laurelwood', one of the prose pieces in *Note-Books of Night*, he talks of how his grandfather and grandmother helped teach him the names of everyday objects. His range of knowledge is one of the many marvellous things about Wilson. In poems like 'Provincetown, 1936' he piled on the detail to good effect:

> Mussels with broken hinges, sea crabs lopped
> Of legs, black razor-clams split double, dried
> Sea-dollars, limpets chivied loose and dropped
> Like stranded dories rolling on their side.

But in the long run not even concrete facts were a sufficient antidote to the poetry of Beauty. Humour was a better safeguard. On the whole, it is the satirical verse which holds up best among Wilson's work. Quite apart from the classic 'The Omelet of A. MacLeish', there are 'The Extrovert of Walden Pond' (with its *trouvé* catch-phrase 'Thoreau was a neuro') and 'The Playwright in Paradise', a minatory ode to the writers of his generation which borrows lines from 'Adonais' to remind them that in Beverly Hills their talents will die young. In these poems Wilson's critical intelligence was at work. If he had possessed comic invention to match his scornful parodic ear, he might have equalled even E. E. Cummings. But 'American Masterpieces' (which makes its only appearance in *Night Thoughts*) shows what Cummings had that Wilson hadn't: in mocking the clichés of Madison Avenue, Wilson can win your allegiance, but Cummings can make you laugh. At the last, Wilson's jokes are not quite funny enough in themselves – they rarely take off into the self-sustaining Empyrean of things you can't help reciting. His humour, like his frankness, ought ideally to have been part of a larger fiction.

Useless to carp. A minor artist Wilson remains. But it ought to be more generally realized that he was a very good minor artist, especially in his poetry. Of course, *Night Thoughts* didn't help. Inflated with juvenilia and senescent academic graffiti even duller than Auden's, the book blurred the outlines of Wilson's achievement – although even here it should be noted that its closing poem, 'The White Sand', is one of Wilson's most affecting things, a despairing celebration of late love so deeply felt that it almost overcomes the sense of strain generated by the internally rhymed elegiacs in which it is cast.

What has worked most damagingly against Wilson's reputation as a poet, however, is his reputation as a critic. It is hard to see how things could be otherwise. As a critical mind, Wilson is so great that we have not yet taken his full measure. He is still so prominent as to be invisible: people think they can know what he said without having to read him. When he is read again, it will soon be found that he saw both sides of most of the arguments which continue to rage about what literature is or ought to be. Among these arguments is the one about modern poetry and its audience. Nobody was more sympathetic than Wilson to the emergence of a difficult, hermetic poetry or better equipped to understand its origins. But equally he was able to keep the issue in perspective. First of all, his standards were traditional in the deepest sense: knowing why Homer, Virgil, Dante, Shakespeare and Pushkin were permanently modern, he knew why most of modern poetry was without the value it claimed for itself. Secondly, he had an unconquerable impulse towards community. All his writings are an expression of it, including his verse. He would have liked to read fully intelligible works while living in an ordered society. As things turned out, the works he admired were not always fully intelligible and the society he lived in was not ordered. But at least in his own creative writings, such as they were, he could try to be clear. So his poems are as they are, and the best of them last well.

JOHN UPDIKE

Wilson's Fiction: A Personal Account

Memoirs of Hecate County came out in 1946; I read a copy borrowed from the Reading, Pennsylvania, public library, where it sat placidly on the open shelves while the book was being banned in New York State. Mere reading must have seemed a mild sin in the Reading of those years; it was a notoriously permissive town, famous for its rackets, its whores and its acquitting juries. In 1946 I was 14. What that slightly sinister volume, a milky green in the original Double-day edition, with the epigraph from Gogol in Russian and a sepia photograph of a three-faced Hecate opposite the title page, meant to me, I can reconstruct imperfectly. Certainly I skipped the pages of French that the curious Mr. Blackburn spouts toward the end, and probably I skimmed the inside-the-book-business ax-grinding of 'The Milhollands and their Damned Soul'. But the long, central story, 'The Princess with the Golden Hair', the heart and scandal of this collection of six 'memoirs', I read, as they say, avidly, my first and to this day most vivid glimpse of sex through the window of fiction.

All of my life I have remembered how Anna, 'as a gesture of affection and respect', held the hero's penis in her hand as they drifted off to sleep; and how Imogen in coitus halted her lover and 'did something special and gentle' that caused her to have her climax first; and how one of the women (I had forgotten which) gazes at the narrator, and through him at the amazed young reader, over the curve of her naked hip. This last image, redolent of the casual intimacy and exposure that adults presumably enjoyed, affected me so powerfully I was surprised, rereading, to discover how brief it is:

. . . once, when I came back into the room, I found her
curled up on the bed and was pleased by her eyes, very
cunning and round – at once agate like marbles and soft like
burrs – looking at me over her hips.

It is Anna, of course, and the emphasis – typical of Wilson's erotic
art – is all on her eyes. The mechanically and psychologically
complicated business of Imogen's backbrace touched me less
memorably, but like the images above it smelled of the real, it
showed sex as a human transaction that did honestly take place,
not in the infinitely elastic wonderland of pornography but on
actual worn furniture, in moods of doubt and hangover, in a muddle
of disillusion and balked comfort: the hero does not omit to let us
know that he found Anna's fond trick of penis-holding 'in the long
run . . . uncomfortable'. There was something dogged and humor-
less and pungent about Wilson's rendition of love: the adjective
'meaty' recurs, spoiling pleasant contexts, and the simile everyone
remembers from *I Thought of Daisy* tells of the heroine's held feet,
'in pale stockings . . . like two little moist cream cheeses encased
in covers of cloth'. Pungent, and savage: I was blinded by the
journal entry, in 'Princess', that begins '——ing in the afternoon,
with the shades down and all her clothes on – different from anything else – rank satisfactory smell like the salt marine tides we come
out of . . .'. And a very naked moment comes in the last story, at
the Blackburns' party, when the hero throws Jo, the third of his
willing fornicatrices, onto the bed full of guests' wraps:

> She put one arm up over her eyes; her legs dangled, like a
> child's, from her knees . . . 'Move forward', I said, and put her
> legs up. Her white thighs and her lower buttocks were
> brutally laid bare; her feet, in silver openwork sandals, were
> pointing in opposite directions.

Of course I could have got this sort of thing, in 1946, from
Erskine Caldwell or John O'Hara, indeed *did* get it from the
Southern California detective fiction of James Cain and Raymond
Chandler; but the sex in these writers was not fortified by Wilson's
conscious intention of bringing European sexual realism into

American fiction at last. The publication of Wilson's notebooks, *The Twenties*, from which the Anna sections of *Hecate County* are taken almost verbatim, show his sexual scorecards mingled as if naively with landscape descriptions and intellectual ruminations and the anecdotes of his rather silly upper-class friends. The original jacket of *Hecate County* describes it as 'the adventures of an egoist among the bedeviled'. America seemed incorrigibly alien to Wilson, though fascinating, and intrinsic to his destiny. Like Dante, he is a tourist *engagé*. The lonely bookish child stares with a frown from the shadows of the Red Bank mansion, where the mother was deaf and the father nervously fragile; the America he perceives seems grim and claustrophobic, though hectic. There is a true whiff of Hell in Hecate County, less in the specific touches of supernatural diabolism with which this utter rationalist quaintly adorned his tales, but in the low ceilings and cheap underwear of the sex idyll, the clothes and neuroses of the copulators. America has always tolerated sex as a joke, as a night's prank in the burlesque theater or fairground tent; but not as a solemn item in life's work inventory. It was Wilson's deadly earnest, his unwinking naturalistic refusal to release us into farce, that made *Hecate County* in all its dignity and high intent the target of a (successful!) prosecution for obscenity. Earnest, but not Ernest Hemingway, who never in his fictional personae shows himself compromised, as this sweating, fumbling hero of Wilson's so often is; Hemingway's heroes make love without baring their bottoms, and the women as well as the men are falsified by a romantic severity, an exemption from the odors and awkwardness that Wilson, with the dogged selfless honesty of a bookworm, presses his own nose, and ours, into with such solemn satisfaction.

Rereading, now, in this liberated age, and in the light of the notebooks, one expects to find the sex tame. And so, in a sense, it is. '——ing' turns out to be, in the unexpurgated journals, merely 'Fucking', rather than the more exotic activity I tried to imagine, and the tender journal accounts of cunnilingus and fellatio* and

---

* '. . . the cool moisture of her lips when she has bent lower for fellatio, so delightful, so curiously different from the warm and mucilaginous

Anna's 'monthlies' did not find their way into even the revised edition of 1959.

In the fiction, Wilson sets down no sexual detail in simple celebration, to please and excite himself, but always to illuminate the social or psychological condition of the two women. The Anna of 'Princess', compared to the confusing love-object of the journals, is admirably coherent, as the product of certain cultural and economic conditions in Brooklyn; how telling, for instance, is her reluctance to be seen naked, as if nudity – to the upper classes an aesthetic proclamation, a refutation of shame – evokes inhibitions having nothing to do with sexual acts, which she performs freely. And how plausibly, if ploddingly, are the clothes of the two women described and made to symbolize their social presences. Such details – seized, we sometimes feel, by a sensibility that doubts its own grasp on the 'real' – lend the factual sexual descriptions a weight, a heat, far from tame.

It is Imogen (her original may be waiting exposure in the unpublished journals of the thirties; married for sixteen years, she seems too old for the narrator at the age he assigns himself, 'on the verge of thirty') who occasions Wilson's subtlest, harshest instances of sexual realism. After two years of yearning, the hero greets their tryst in a mood of nervous lassitude. The very perfection of her body distances her – 'I found that I was expressing admiration of her points as if she were some kind of museum piece' – and her eager lubricity, 'making things easy for the entrant with a honey-sweet sleek profusion', dulls his triumph: 'She became, in fact, so smooth and open that after a moment I could hardly feel her . . . I went on and had a certain disappointment, for, with the brimming of female fluid, I felt even less sensation; but – gently enough – I came, too.' Gently enough, the failure of an overprepared, ideal

---

moisture of ordinary intercourse – the incredible-feeling caress, gently up and down, until the delightful brimming swelling of pleasure seems to make it flow really in waves which fill her darling woman's mouth.' The passage, so lyrical, goes on however to observe 'the man a little embarrassed, feels a little bit differently about her mouth, but affectionately kisses her'.

love to connect is masterfully anatomized, and movingly contrasted with his tawdry, harried affair with Anna, that involves him with criminal types and gives him gonorrhea. One's breath is snatched to see, in the journals, the patrician, pontifical Wilson led by sex to the edge of the abyss of poverty, its diseases, its tangled familial furies, its hopeless anonymity. He did not fall in. The last story of *Hecate County*, surreal and troubled, prefigures the hero's marriage to Jo Gates, a well-off, cheerful 'Western girl' like Margaret Canby, whom Wilson married in 1930, closing out the decade, and clamping down on 'a feeling that, fond though I was of Margaret and well though we got along, we did not have enough in common'.

The journals make clear more abundantly than the novella how much Wilson had loved Anna, how fully she satisfied him and gave him his deferred manhood. 'The Princess with the Golden Hair' is a love-poem to her and one of the best of his writing generation's obligatory love-poems to the lower classes.

> Yet for them the depression was always going on like a flood that swept away their houses ... and the attitudes, I knew, that I assumed to myself and in my conversations with others meant nothing in that bare room in Brooklyn where Anna and her garment-worker cousin were so sober and anxious and pale.

Like Thornton Wilder's *Heaven's My Destination*, 'Princess' is a generous aberration, a visit to the underworld by a member of the last predominantly Wasp generation of writers, the last that conceived of itself as an aristocracy. Wilson's portrait of this one slum-child lives by her light, the 'something so strong and instinctive that it could outlive the hurts and infections, the defilements, among which we lived'. The fiction she inhabits, as its true princess, overtops the flanking Gothic vignettes (though 'Ellen Terhune' has its authenticity, and the last story a wrenched pain) and makes plausible Wilson's insistence that *Memoirs of Hecate County* was his favorite among his many books. His fiction, generally cluttered, savoring of the worked-up, of collected details moved by *force majeure* of the writer's mind, here finds a theme that moves *him*. Sex was his one way *in*, into the America to which his response, however much he wished it otherwise, was to reach for anaesthesia, whether found in books or bottles. Imogen, in this respect, is a better metaphor for America than Anna; her flamboyant costumes and greedy orgasms serve the same narcissism, reflect the same blank passion to succeed; in her richly, ironically particularized and over-furnished setting, she ends as a comic vision, empty but not un-lovable, a gaudy suburban witch, in a land where, after 1946, Hecate Counties would spread and multiply and set the new cultural tone. Freud more than Marx would bias our lives; the suburban home would replace the city street as the theatre of hopes; private fulfillment and not public justice would set the pace of the pursuit of happiness. Until the mid-sixties this remained true, and Wilson, writing out of notebooks kept in the twenties, foretold it, casting his fiction in the coming mode, of sexual candor, dark sardonic fantasy, and confessional fragment.

I read *I Thought of Daisy* years later, and there is some inverse pro-gression in this, for it is the more rounded novel, more thoroughly intended and unified than the six disparate 'memoirs', though in the earlier book too Wilson has composed his narrative in a series of – in this case, five – discrete panels. Here too is the first-person narrator given to essayistic asides and hopeful of unriddling America through the person of a female native less intellectual and well-born than himself. Again, the book is liveliest in its landscapes and erotic scenes, and relatively leaden in its sociological disquisitions; the presentation, for instance, of Hugo Bamman as the type of twenties radical seems 'blocked in' with large shadows and thick lines, and lifts free into specificity only in the mad moment when Hugo apparently embarks on a boat to Afghanistan straight from a taxi containing the hero and Daisy. The hero tells us that he is under Hugo's sway, but in fact seems, as narrator–analyst, on top of him from the start. In his introduction to the revised edition of 1953 Wilson confesses how 'schematic' *Daisy* is, and claims to be 'rather appalled by the rigor with which I sacrificed to my plan of five symphonic movements what would normally have been the line of the story'. The character of Rita, based upon that of Edna St. Vincent Millay, especially resisted his scheme, dominating sections where she was meant to be subordinate, and yet remaining more mysterious, in her involvement with the narrator, than she should have been.

Yet for all Wilson's strictures upon himself the book has much that is lovely about it, beginning with the title. The phrase, 'I thought of Daisy', occurs in each section but the last, and here, oddly, in the excursion to Coney Island that is closely derived from an account in the journals of such a trip with 'Florence', Wilson fails to transcribe a note of what may be the original inspiration:

> postcards: American flag with silver tinsel inscription – 'I thought of you at Coney Island'.

The twenties journals throw considerable light upon the genesis of this novel. Wilson began it in 1926 or '27, and rewrote it drastically in a beach house in California, near the home of Margaret Canby, late in 1928. He confided to Maxwell Perkins that *Axel's Castle*, which he was carrying forward simultaneously, 'being literary criticism, is easier to do, and in the nature of a relief, from *Daisy*'. To John Peale Bishop he wrote that 'it was to be a pattern of ideas and all to take place, as to a great extent it does, on the plane of intelligence – and when I came to write the actual story, this had the effect of involving me in a certain amount of falsified psychology'. He got the book off to Perkins early in 1929, and in the midst of his near-breakdown later that winter, within the sanitorium at Clifton Springs, New York, he went over the page proofs. The period of crisis in which he completed this novel is also the time of his romance with Anna, and in his journals he was writing, without knowing it, his one other extended fiction. After 1929 a certain abdication and consolidation took place; he got a divorce and remarried, forsook Anna, and settled on criticism as his métier. As a critic, he has said all that need be said against his own first novel. What needs to be added is how good, if ungainly, *Daisy* is, how charmingly and intelligently she tells of the speakeasy days of a Greenwich Village as red and cozy as a valentine, of lamplit islands where love and ambition and drunkenness* bloomed all at once. The fiction writer in Wilson was real, and his displacement a real loss.

In 1953 he stated that *Daisy* was 'written much under the influence of Proust and Joyce'. Though the novel constitutes a kind of portrait of the artist as a young man, and gives New York a little of the street-guide specificity Joyce gave Dublin, the influence of Proust is far more conspicuous. The *longueurs*, the central notion of changing perspectives and 'intermittences of the heart', the importance of party scenes, the contraction of some intervals of time (e.g. the hero's European trip) into mere summary while other moments are expansively and repeatedly treated, the search for 'laws' of behavior and perception, the mock-scientific rigor with which aesthetic and subjective impressions are examined, the musical, wide-ranging speculativeness – all this is Proustian. Wilson, indeed, was one of the few Americans intellectually energetic enough to put Proust's example to work. This example fused surface and thought, commonplace reality with a 'symphonic' prose of inexhaustible refinement. Wilson had Proust's love for whatever could be assimilated to his mind. Daisy, with her cream-cheese feet and her way of saying 'um' for 'them', is not as floral an apparition as Odette, nor do Wilson's glimpses of our hard seaboard resonate like the steeples at Martinville; but there is that same rapt reception of the glimpse as a symbol:

> Then suddenly I had almost caught my breath – I had been curiously moved by the sight of a single, solitary street lamp on the Staten Island shore. It had merely shed a loose and whitish radiance over a few feet of the baldish road of some dark, thinly settled suburb. Above it, there had loomed an

---

* There is quite a lot of drunkenness in Wilson's scant fiction. The third chapter of *Daisy* and the last of *Hecate County* both show the gradual derangement of the narrator within 'That enchanted country of drink that was the world one had been young in, in the twenties!' The funniest and most harrowing bibulous episode occupies the 1934 sketch, 'What to Do Till the Doctor Comes (From the Diary of a Drinker-Out)', reprinted in *The American Earthquake*, with three other pieces of reportorial 'fiction'.

abundant and disorderly tree. But there was America, I had
felt with emotion – there under that lonely suburban street
lamp, there in that raw and livid light!

The young hero, coming out onto Professor Grosbeake's glassed-in
porch at Princeton after an evening spent in intoxicating, idealistic
conversation, feels the winter chill mix with his mentor's abstract
theology:

> ... and as I took leave of Grosbeake – gazing out through the
> glass at the pavement lightly dappled with leaves and the dark
> grass glittering with wet – my mind bemused with a vision of
> God as a vast crystal fixing its symmetry from a liquified
> universe – I felt a delicious delicacy of iciness, glossy fall-leaf
> slivers and black rain-glinting glass.

Such interpenetration of mind and matter is surely a great theme,
and few Americans were better qualified to dramatize it than
Wilson, with his polymathic curiosity and his pungent earthiness,
his autocratic intellect and initially quite benign and humble
willingness to sniff out the grubbiest lessons that mysterious America
could set for him.

In its final printing in his uniform edition, *Daisy* is bound with a
short story, 'Galahad', composed by Wilson in the early twenties.
Its adolescent hero, Hart Foster, about to assume leadership of his
prep-school Young Men's Christian Association, is nearly seduced
by the sister of a friend, who takes off her clothes and gets into bed
with him.

> As she bent over him for a moment, Hart had a glimpse of
> her firm round breasts; he was surprised to find them so big:
> he had always supposed that girls' breasts were little low
> dotted things.

The ingenuously confessed surprise is Wilsonian, as is the genuine
ethical struggle of the boy upon his return to the school. He does
not lightly dismiss the Puritan morality, nor the opposed morality
that follows the revelation that 'this was the real Barbara, this

solid living body! – not merely the face at the top of a dress that one knew in ordinary life'. He plays truant from the school to visit her, and faced with her again becomes 'a helpless child' before 'the terrible prestige of her sexual experience'. She advises him to return, and he does. The story commands considerable suspense, as it presents in open conflict, near the outset of their long conjoined career, the polarities of Wilson's self-education: the conscientious humanist and the anarchic concupiscent. Especially vivid for me, in 'Galahad', was the train ride down from New England toward New York, a ride I often took in my own student days, gazing like Hart Foster through the gliding windows 'with a kind of morbid relish for every dry winter meadow mottled with melting snow, for every long flat factory building, for every black ice-glazed stream, for every hard square-angled town with its hollow-looking boxlike houses . . .'. Wilson is peculiarly a poet of this wintry, skeletal, Northeastern landscape, and his journals of the twenties end with a glorious display of Connecticut snowbound as the thirties begin.

Why did the author of 'Galahad' produce so little else in the way of short fiction? Why did the author of *Daisy* not go on to become the American Proust? Why, for that matter, did the best-selling memoirist of *Hecate County* not follow this most favorite of his books with something similar? One answer, no doubt, is drably practical: no one much encouraged him to write fiction. A negative practical consequence of *Hecate County*'s *succès de scandale* was Wilson's later run-in with the federal government over unpaid taxes, and the truculent anti-Americanism of *The Cold War and the Income Tax*. He was as astonished to discover that America's laws applied to him as Hart Foster was to discover that breasts were big; and took the fact less kindly. Another answer may lie in the nature of his great intelligence: he could extrapolate from facts but not much budge them. An immensely mobile gatherer of information, he wrote no fiction without a solidly planted autobiographical base, and his fantasy, when it intervenes, as in the side-pieces of *Hecate County*, seems clumsy and harsh. He drew on journal notations and didn't much trust his memory, that great sifter of significance; forgetfulness, the subconscious shaper of many a fiction, had no place in his equipment. And a third answer, of course, is that the fiction-writer went underground and greatly enriched the reporter, lent the critic his bracing directness and energy, co-authored the plays and vivacious self-interviews of Wilson's antic moods, and lay behind the flamboyance of those feats of reading and startling acquisitions of expertise that kept lengthening the shelf of his squat, handy volumes. He worked up subjects like the Dead Sea scrolls and the Iroquois Indians much as popular novelists like Irving Stone and James Michener appropriate Hawaii or Michelangelo, to turn them into books. The comparison is well-meant: Wilson wrote in the marketplace; he aimed to become a writer in a professional sense unimaginable to most serious young men now; the scholar and drudge within him served a poet of reality.

EDMUND WILSON'S BOOKS

❧

A Checklist

The Undertaker's Garland (with John Peale Bishop) (poems and stories), New York, 1922.

Discordant Encounters: Plays and Dialogues, New York, 1926.

I Thought of Daisy (novel), New York, 1929; London, 1952; etc.

Poets, Farewell! (poems and essays), New York, 1929.

Axel's Castle: A Study in the Imaginative Literature of 1870–1930 (criticism), New York, 1930; London, 1961; etc.

The American Jitters: A Year of the Slump (social criticism), New York, 1932.

Travels in Two Democracies (on U.S.A. and U.S.S.R.: dialogues, essays, a story), New York, 1936.

This Room and This Gin and These Sandwiches: Three Plays, New York, 1937.

The Triple Thinkers: Ten Essays on Literature, New York, 1938; London, 1938; etc. (Re-issued with two additional essays, 1918.)

To the Finland Station: A Study in the Writing and Acting of History, New York, 1940; London, 1940; etc.

The Boys in the Back Room: Notes on California Novelists, San Francisco, 1941.

The Wound and the Bow: Seven Studies in Literature, Boston, 1941; London, 1942; etc.

Note-Books of Night (poems, essays, parody), San Francisco, 1942; London, 1945.

Memoirs of Hecate County (stories), New York, 1946; London, 1951; etc.

Europe Without Baedeker: Sketches Among the Ruins of Italy, Greece and England, New York, 1947; London, 1948; etc.

The Little Blue Light: A Play in Three Acts, New York, 1950; London, 1951.

Classics and Commercials: A Literary Chronicle of the Forties, New York, 1950; London, 1951; etc.

The Shores of Light: A Literary Chronicle of the Twenties, New York, 1952; London, 1952; etc.

Five Plays, London, 1954; New York, 1954.

The Scrolls from the Dead Sea, New York, 1955; London, 1955; etc.

Red, Black, Blond and Olive (travel book; the contents of *Travels in Two Democracies* plus essays on Zuñi and Haiti), New York, 1956; London, 1956.

A Piece of My Mind: Reflections at Sixty, New York, 1956; London, 1957.

The American Earthquake: A Documentary of the Twenties and Thirties (reprinted journalism: social criticism), New York, 1958; London, 1958; etc.

Apologies to the Iroquois (historical survey), New York, 1960; London, 1960.

Night Thoughts (poems), New York, 1961; London, 1962.

Patriotic Gore: Studies in the Literature of the American Civil War, New York, 1962; London, 1962; etc.

The Cold War and the Income Tax: A Protest (social criticism), New York, 1963; London, 1964.

O Canada: An American's Notes on Canadian Culture, New York, 1965; London, 1967.

The Bit Between My Teeth: A Literary Chronicle of 1950–1965, New York, 1965; London, 1966.

A Prelude: Landscapes, Characters and Conversations from the Earlier Years of My Life, New York, 1967; London, 1967.

The Duke of Palermo and Other Plays with an Open Letter to Mike Nichols, New York, 1969; London, 1969.

The Dead Sea Scrolls 1947–1969 (the contents of *The Scrolls from the Dead Sea* with subsequent material), New York, 1969; London, 1969.

Upstate: Records and Recollections of Northern New York (regional history, family history, autobiography, etc., etc.), New York, 1971.

Edmund Wilson also did a good deal of editing; without attempting to list every book with his name on the title-page, we should be aware of two major contributions, viz.:

The Crack-Up: With Other Uncollected Pieces (material by, and about, F. Scott Fitzgerald), New York, 1945; London, 1947.

The Shock of Recognition: The Development of Literature in the United States Recorded by the Men Who Made It (literary and social history), New York, 1943; London, 1956.

Acknowledgements

The following excerpts are reprinted with the permission of Farrar, Straus & Giroux, Inc.: from THE SHORES OF LIGHT by Edmund Wilson, Copyright 1952 by Edmund Wilson; from CLASSICS AND COMMERCIALS by Edmund Wilson, Copyright 1950 by Edmund Wilson, Copyright renewed © 1978 by Elena Wilson; from THE AMERICAN EARTHQUAKE by Edmund Wilson, Copyright © 1958 by Edmund Wilson; from NIGHT THOUGHTS by Edmund Wilson, Copyright © 1953, 1961 by Edmund Wilson; from MEMOIRS OF HECATE COUNTY by Edmund Wilson, Copyright © 1942, 1943, 1946, © 1959 by Edmund Wilson, copyright renewed © 1974 by Elena Wilson; from I THOUGHT OF DAISY by Edmund Wilson, Copyright © 1929, 1953 by Edmund Wilson; from THE TWENTIES by Edmund Wilson, edited with an introduction by Leon Edel, Copyright © 1975 by Elena Wilson, Executrix of the Estate of Edmund Wilson; from THE DUKE OF PALERMO AND OTHER PLAYS by Edmund Wilson, Copyright © 1930, 1967, 1969 by Edmund Wilson; from APOLOGIES TO THE IROQUOIS by Edmund Wilson, Copyright © 1959, 1960 by Edmund Wilson; from TO THE FINLAND STATION by Edmund Wilson, Copyright 1940 by Edmund Wilson; from A WINDOW ON RUSSIA by Edmund Wilson, Copyright © 1943, 1944, 1952, 1957, 1965, 1967, 1969, 1970, 1971, 1972 by Edmund Wilson, Copyright renewed © 1971, 1972 by Edmund Wilson; from A PIECE OF MY MIND by Edmund Wilson, Copyright © 1956 by Edmund Wilson, Copyright © 1956 by the American Jewish Committee; from THE SHOCK OF RECOGNITION by Edmund Wilson, Copyright 1943 by Doubleday, Doran and Company, Inc., Copyright 1955 by Edmund Wilson; from THE BIT BETWEEN MY TEETH by Edmund Wilson, Copyright © 1939, 1940, 1947, 1950, 1951, 1952, 1953, 1956, 1957, 1958, 1959, 1960, 1961, 1962, 1963, 1965 by Edmund Wilson; from RED, BLACK, BLOND AND OLIVE by Edmund Wilson, Copyright © 1956 by Edmund Wilson; from A PRELUDE by Edmund Wilson, Copyright © 1967 by Edmund Wilson; from THE TRIPLE THINKERS by Edmund Wilson, Copyright 1938, 1948 by Edmund Wilson, Copyright renewed 1956, 1971 by Edmund Wilson and 1976 by Elena Wilson, Executrix of the Estate of Edmund Wilson.

The excerpts from AXEL'S CASTLE by Edmund Wilson, Copyright 1930 by

177

ACKNOWLEDGEMENTS

Edmund Wilson, are reprinted by permission of Charles Scribner's Sons. The excerpts from NOTE-BOOKS OF NIGHT *by Edmund Wilson, Copyright 1942 by Edmund Wilson, are reprinted by permission of Secker & Warburg Ltd, London, and Farrar, Straus & Giroux, Inc., New York. The excerpt from* PATRIOTIC GORE *by Edmund Wilson, Copyright © 1962 by Edmund Wilson, is reprinted by permission of André Deutsch Ltd, London, and Farrar, Straus & Giroux, Inc., New York.*

The excerpt from THE LETTERS OF F. SCOTT FITZGERALD, *edited by Andrew Turnbull, is reprinted by permission of The Bodley Head Ltd, London, and Charles Scribner's Sons, New York. The excerpt from* KING LOG *by Geoffrey Hill, 1968, is reprinted by permission of André Deutsch Ltd, London, and Dufour Editions, Inc., Chester Springs, Pa. 19425, U.S.A. The excerpt from* HIGH WINDOWS *by Philip Larkin is reprinted by permission of Faber and Faber Ltd, London, and Farrar, Straus & Giroux, Inc., New York. The quotation from* CHURCH GOING *by Philip Larkin is reprinted from* THE LESS DECEIVED *by permission of The Marvell Press, England. The excerpt from* STUDIES IN WORDS *by C. S. Lewis is reprinted by permission of Cambridge University Press. The selection from 'Harriet' from* NOTEBOOK *by Robert Lowell, Copyright © 1967, 1968, 1969, 1970 by Robert Lowell, is reprinted by permission of Faber and Faber Ltd, London, and Farrar, Straus & Giroux, Inc., New York. The excerpt from* THE COLLECTED POEMS OF LOUIS MACNEICE *is reprinted by permission of Faber and Faber Ltd, London, and Oxford University Press, New York. The excerpt from* THE COLLECTED POEMS OF WALLACE STEVENS *is reprinted by permission of Faber and Faber Ltd, London, and Alfred A. Knopf, Inc., New York. The excerpts from* GRANITE AND RAINBOW *and* THE DEATH OF THE MOTH AND OTHER ESSAYS *by Virginia Woolf are reprinted by permission of the author's literary estate, The Hogarth Press, London, and Harcourt Brace Jovanovich, Inc., New York. The excerpts from* THE COLLECTED POEMS OF W. B. YEATS *are reprinted by permission of M. B. Yeats, Miss Anne Yeats, and Macmillan, London and Basingstoke, and Macmillan Publishing Co., Inc., New York, copyright 1919 and 1928 by Macmillan Publishing Co., Inc., renewed 1947 and 1956 by Bertha Georgie Yeats.*

Index